F1

THROUGH THE EYES OF
DAMON HILL
Inside the World of Formula One

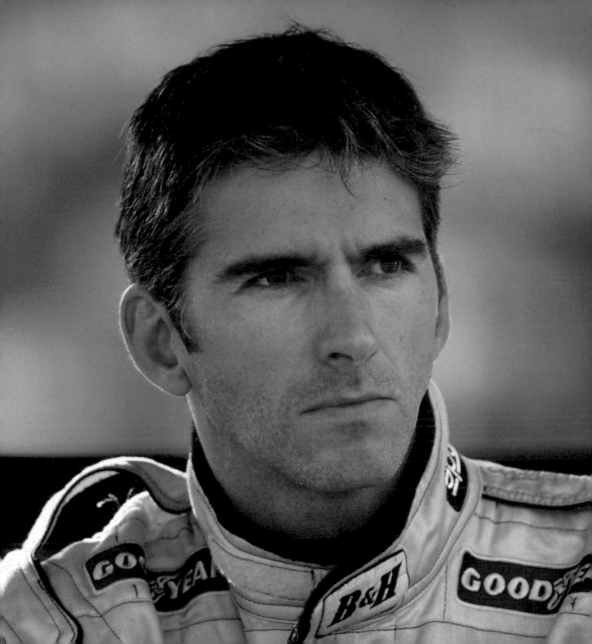

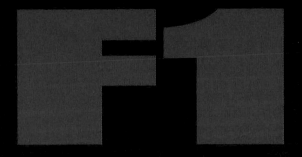

F1

THROUGH THE EYES OF
DAMON HILL
Inside the World of Formula One

Photographs by Keith Sutton

Little, Brown and Company

BOSTON · NEW YORK · LONDON

F1

THROUGH THE EYES OF **DAMON HILL**

chapter one
ORIGINS

chapter two
EXPECTATION

chapter four
AMBITION

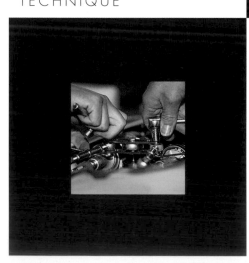

chapter three
TECHNIQUE

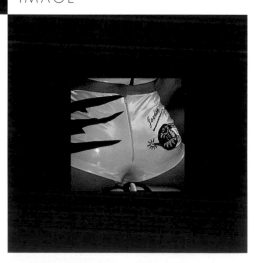

chapter five
IMAGE

CONTENTS

chapter six
RIVALRY

chapter seven
PRIVACY

chapter nine
FEAR

chapter eight
WINNING

chapter ten
FUTURE

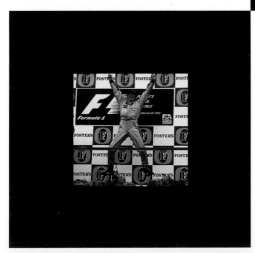

THROUGH THE EYES OF **DAMON HILL**

When I agreed to write another book about my experiences in the extraordinary world of Formula One, I thought there was no way I was going to give myself all the added work and stress on top of my first season with the Benson and Hedges Jordan Mugen-Honda Team merely for the publisher's advance. So I thought I'd just get the best photographer, make it look really nice by using the best designer and then knock out a few words which nobody would read because they would be too distracted by the stylish layout and pictures.

Only, when it came to it, I just couldn't do that, because there was so much I wanted to explain about my job, my background, my first win for Jordan, the lifestyle, the fans, fear, image, ambition and rivalry . . . you get the idea.

So here it is. A book about all of that. But you can just look at the pictures if you prefer . . .

Damon Hill
November 1998

There was a bittersweet taste to my championship-winning year in 1996, because I had already lost my job with the Williams team when I lifted the title. There was nothing to be gained by moping about being bumped out of Williams so I made it my objective to get a seat at McLaren, which was clearly going to be the best place to go.

Why was I so certain of that? Simple – Adrian Newey would be designing the car and they were a solid, well-established team. In my mind, those two facts alone were enough to convince me that McLaren would be the best car in 1998 and they would present me with my best chance of winning the championship again.

I had several approaches at the end of 1996, including one from Eddie Jordan, but I was hedging my bets. I wanted to find a team where I could be happy for a year, hopefully be competitive and then get myself into McLaren for the following season. At least, that was the plan, and that was where Tom Walkinshaw came in.

I like Tom. He has a reputation for being tough. He is a no-nonsense businessman and he doesn't muck about. He offered me a contract which didn't tie me in for two or five years. It was a single year, exactly what I wanted. His attitude was 'give me a year to prove myself and, at the same time, you show me what you can do in my team' and that was fine with me. It was an honest approach from him and, I thought, it gave us both what we wanted. He had the world champion, I had a one-year deal.

Something could have happened at Arrows if Tom had got a good engine. He had made the move to using Bridgestone tyres, which I felt would be better. Tyres are absolutely crucial to how the cars work and everything I had heard about the Bridgestones was positive – and also Arrows had done a lot of the development work for them. Rather ironically, my enthusiasm led to McLaren pursuing the Bridgestone route because, during my negotiations with McLaren, Adrian was asking me about the Bridgestones and I told him he had to get them. So he did. Unfortunately, I was not there to enjoy them, but I'm getting ahead of the story.

When I joined Arrows in 1997, I was confident that this was a team on the move, one that was going to improve quickly. I thought the Yamaha engine would work a lot better than it did, largely on the basis of promises that were made before the season, and I put a lot of faith in Tom's ability to turn things around. I had it in mind that if I couldn't get myself into McLaren, then Arrows could be a place where I could think about staying.

"I made it my objective to get a seat at McLaren, which was clearly going to be the best place to go."

Looking back, perhaps I put too much faith in Tom and the team, because things did not turn out that well. We had one fantastic day in Hungary, when I overtook Michael Schumacher and came within a few miles of winning, but other than that, it was clear to me that I should move on.

I had kept in contact with Ron Dennis, McLaren's managing director, and spoken to him regularly throughout the season. He knew how much I wanted to drive for his team and how keen I was to do a deal. Talking about it is one thing, though. Finalising it is quite another.

I left Arrows because I didn't think they would be competitive, and that has always been the most important factor governing my decision about which team to drive for. As far as I was concerned, the most important thing was to get myself back in the frame and that is why I had my sights set on McLaren.

Throughout 1997 I was hoping Arrows would come good, but also that I could work a situation where I could get into McLaren. I was in regular contact with Ron Dennis, trying to find out if there would be a place for me in the team.

It is just about impossible to keep anything secret in Formula One and, before too long, it became known that I was available. Soon, people were falling over themselves to talk to me and I had offers from a lot of teams. The only problem was that none of them was McLaren.

By then, it was evident that the performance of the Arrows was not going ahead fast enough to give me a chance of winning races for them in the following year. That was clear as soon as Tom failed to get the Honda engine. For a long while he expected to do the deal, but another team tied it up before him – Jordan.

"It is just about impossible to keep anything secret in Formula One and, before too long, it became known that I was available."

Tough,
Tom Walkinshaw

Because I had turned down Eddie Jordan in 1997, I had lost contact with him. I had been contacted by Alain Prost and Peter Sauber, but my primary goal was to get a drive at McLaren because I knew that would put me into a championship-winning situation. All these discussions were on the boil and then Hungary happened.

It was a fantastic race for me, the sort of day when nearly everything goes right. I qualified well, got into second place at the start, then I overtook Michael Schumacher and after that it was a case of driving off into the distance. For lap after lap, the feeling was fantastic and it looked certain that I would win Arrows' first-ever Grand Prix until, a few miles from home, the car stuck in gear.

I still came second, though, which got everybody's attention. For me, it was a moment of glory, the peak of my year. In fact, it was the peak of everything at Arrows and it coincided with the time when a decision had to be made about where I would go. I was waiting to see what McLaren would say, still hoping that we could sort out a deal and end all the speculation.

Back to the front again

At the same time, I still had to make up my mind about what to tell the other teams, because they had made me good offers, and here I was, putting myself in a position where I was waiting on McLaren to jump my way.

The problem when you are negotiating in situations like this is that you can end up boxed in, with no position from which to negotiate. You always need to have options available to you and that was the danger I faced. If I told the others that I wasn't interested, Ron could have waited until the cows came home before making me an offer. He knew I wanted the drive and he could have exploited that by delaying his decision and playing me off the other drivers he had in mind. I could have ended up having nowhere to go.

It was obvious that I had to put pressure on him, and that meant I had a very stressful time knowing that this was a window of opportunity that would not last very long. I was being offered fantastic opportunities at other teams (or I could have stayed at Arrows), but I wanted to go to the most competitive one, naturally.

Then Hungary happened and, after that, just about every team boss in the sport got on the phone to me. The last one was Eddie, who rang four days after everybody else. The first thing I said to him was 'You're the last one to call.' He said, 'I didn't think there was any chance you would be interested.' At least we started off with a laugh, which was exactly what I needed at that time.

"I'm not motivated by money, but equally that is one of the ways drivers are ranked in the sport"

Things were not going well with McLaren. I had met with Ron Dennis, and he seemed keen for me to join the team. Then I got an offer from McLaren – and it took me by surprise.

During my discussions with Ron, I had made it clear that there were certain things I expected. I'm not motivated by money, but equally that is one of the ways drivers are ranked in the sport, and if you offer to drive for nothing then that is your perceived worth as a Formula One driver. I didn't want to break his bank by any means, but I wanted to be sure that he was as committed to me as I would be to his team and, as he was wont to repeat, 'money is not a problem'. Additionally, he knew very well what was I being paid to drive by Tom Walkinshaw.

I tend not to overstate my worth. If anything, I'm more self-effacing, but the facts are that I am a world champion and I expected to be paid a retainer that reflected that. I also expected to be treated as well as the other driver in the team because I felt I was at least as good as anybody in Formula One.

He took all my points on board and said there would be no problem with any of them. Then, when he finally got back to me, his offer was way below what we had discussed. For one thing, he wanted me to accept a contract that said I only got paid if I won races. There were no bonuses for scoring points, nothing for coming second or third and nothing if I was winning a race when the car failed. And that happened a lot to McLaren in the 1997 season,

A brilliant second – ah, well . . .

McLaren - no surprises

Mild-mannered genius, Adrian Newey

when the Mercedes engine proved unreliable. The bottom line was that I could turn up to races, get pole position, lead the race for all but one lap, then have the car break down and I would walk away without being paid a penny.

In fact, the contract that I was offered would have meant me earning less money than my team-mate, who I was told would have been Mika Hakkinen. Ron is very close to Mika, and he has been ever since Hakkinen survived a massive crash while driving a McLaren in Adelaide in 1995. Although Ron prides himself on never favouring one driver over another, I had the distinct impression that, if I drove for him, it would be as Hakkinen's deputy. There was no way I could accept that.

I have nothing against Mika. He is a very fast driver with a lot of talent, and I would have been quite happy to have been in a team with him, but I was not going to be his support act. At the time I was talking to Ron about going to McLaren, I had won 21 Grands Prix and a world championship; Mika had never so much as won a Formula One race, yet he was the guy who was going to be earning more money. To me, that would have been getting off on the wrong foot.

One other worrying concern was that he would not talk beyond a one-year deal. I took this to suggest that I would just be warming up the seat for Michael Schumacher, something else I was not prepared to do.

"I had won 21 Grands Prix and
a world championship"

Along with many other things, it gave me the distinct impression that he was actually reluctant to give up what he had. I was working hard to get a place but, for marketing reasons and out of loyalty, I don't think he ever wanted to change things around with his drivers. Mercedes, who make their engines, and West, McLaren's main sponsor, were happy with David Coulthard and Mika Hakkinen's image and I was even told the pair were popular with Mercedes because they looked German! There was not a lot I could do about that – another one for the 'strange but true' Formula One story collection.

The more I thought about it, the more I realised that Ron only wanted to give people the impression that he had negotiated with me, and that it was I who had scuppered the deal. Ron presented me with an offer that he knew I was not going to accept and then, when I turned them down, he was able to shrug his shoulders and blame me. Whatever else you might think of him, there's no denying that Ron Dennis is one of the most manipulative operators in the sport.

Adrian Newey, the man whom I had wanted to follow to McLaren, was doing his bit, pushing for me and encouraging those around him to jump on the Hill bandwagon, but the time came to call a halt. Adrian was new to the team and I did not want him to be in a position where he would jeopardise the start of his career with them. Things had not turned out the way I had hoped, but Adrian still

"I came very close to joining Prost, because I like Alain and I respect him enormously."

had a fantastic opportunity and, as I imagined he would, he did a great job with his first McLaren design.

So that was it. I told Ron that I could not accept his offer and he didn't seem that surprised. I would have been in a weak position within the team to start with and, although I have been given a lot of criticism for my decision, I am happy with it. If I had gone to McLaren, I would not have been happy and I would not have had the relationship of trust that any driver needs. I had spent so long trying to get to that team and I had had so many conversations and made so many plans, but now was the time to let it go. Nevertheless, I put down the telephone to Ron and said to myself: 'Hill, what have you done?'

Still, there was a major decision to be made and I had to be rational. With McLaren out of the way, I had some good offers to look at. Sauber had offered me a substantial deal, but I was not convinced the car would be competitive, and I turned down that offer first of all. That left me three choices – Tom Walkinshaw, Jordan and Prost. Tom did not have a competitive engine sorted out, so that knocked him out of the running, and initially I was very attracted to Alain's team. Indeed, I came very close to joining Prost, because I like Alain and I respect him enormously. They had Bridgestone tyres and the Peugeot engine, both of which looked good on paper, and there seemed to be a lot more enthusiasm about the place since Alain had taken it over.

The decision is made . . .
Prost reads all about it

Window shopping

I had one big problem with the whole thing, though. I was very uncomfortable about being the only 'rosbif' in a French team and, when I voiced these concerns, I was not given any reassurance by Alain that my fears were unfounded. Maybe I was being paranoid, because I am sure all the people at Prost are perfectly nice, but believe me, when you have been through some experiences in Formula One,

that's enough to make you look at every aspect of every deal with a very fine-tooth comb. I stacked it up, thought about it, and I knew I would not be comfortable.

Alain was very upset and he made it clear to various people, including the French Press. That took me by surprise, because I had not expected him to be so bitter and so

public with his feelings. We had been team-mates and he is a man I admire a hell of a lot, but he should have dealt with it better. It was all a bit of sour grapes.

Amid everything else that he said to the journalists, Alain came out with the old line about me only being interested in money. It's an easy thing to throw into conversation and it sounds like he has taken the moral high ground, and that I am mercenary. In fact, Alain got his facts wrong. There was no justification in what he said, because there was very little difference between the retainer he was offering me and the amount I took from Eddie. Both of them offered me a lot less than Peter Sauber had done and Alain's offer was barely half the sum that Tom had offered me. So much for only looking at the bottom line.

I wanted to be happy with the money, but that was not what made up my mind for me. The decision came down to security and competitiveness and, as I thought it over, I could not get over the big problem that Alain was going to have to face – his team had never built a car.

Jordan, on the other hand, seemed to have everything going for it. Eddie's approach to the sport is healthy and this has rubbed off on the rest of the team. They want to be competitive and they are desperate to win their first Grand Prix, but they are not going to lose their sense of humour.

If proof of that were needed, it came with his initial approach to me. Everybody knew that, in 1996, Eddie had made me an offer, but I had turned it down because I just

**A marriage made
in the heavens**

19

wanted a one-year deal. That was why he took his time over coming back to me in 1997 – he thought I might turn him down again.

Eventually, Eddie put himself in the frame, but it was late in the day and by then I had almost ruled him out. I had to put a timescale on making the decision, because I didn't want the whole saga dragging on until the end of the year, and when Eddie first spoke to me, I doubted there was time to meet all the people we would need to speak to in order to get a deal done – team personnel, sponsors, his people, my people. Then, I had some good luck.

After the Italian Grand Prix in Monza, I was planning to get a lift back to England in Tom Walkinshaw's plane. The problem was that, by the time I got to the airport, Tom had already left. I was stranded until, like a good Samaritan, Eddie appeared to offer me a lift back and, as good fortune would have it, all the key people were on board from the team and from Gallaher, the tobacco company who sponsor Jordan through their Benson & Hedges brand.

We didn't do the deal in mid-air – that really would be a dramatic story – but we did make a lot more progress than I could have possibly expected. By the time I got off the plane, Eddie had made me an exciting offer and the people around him had backed everything up. In such a way, Formula One conducts its life – private jets, clandestine meetings and last-minute deals.

**The might of
Mugen-Honda**

Nothing between them

Still, it was a big decision. I took a long time analysing all the factors in all the offers from all the teams. Every single one had 75% of the ingredients but 25% was not there. There was always something missing. Jordan, for instance, were running on Goodyear tyres rather than Bridgestones, and that might have proved to be a problem. A little while

later, they tried to get Bridgestones, but Benetton got there instead and the chance had gone. Goodyear had announced they were pulling out at the end of 1998, so I had worries about their commitment. As things turned out, they put in a fantastic effort to close the gap on their Japanese competitors.

My feeling was that Jordan could continue where they had left off the previous year, knocking on the door of the top four. They seemed to have made a lot of steps forward, with a new wind tunnel and equipment in place, and they seemed well established at a certain level in Formula One. The snag with that situation was that they had lost the Peugeot deal, so they needed a new supplier, and there was a feeling that the Honda engine was not as powerful as the Peugeot.

Above all those fears, though, there was excitement running through my veins. Honda appealed to me because, underneath all that heavy industry, they are a racing organisation. The way they go about racing comes from the heart and, when they put their mind to it, there are very few companies in the world who can put as much into the sport. What they need is for somebody to give them that spark, the desire, and then they are capable of delivering the best machinery to get results. This would be Jordan's opportunity.

Of course, they make cars, but at the same time, there are people throughout the company who love and value racing. It's a completely different attitude from a company like Ford, who make cars and also do some racing on the side to keep up their profile. Honda are more like Ferrari

DAMON HILL

and, like them, they have the potential to be a formidable force – if they put their collective minds to it.

If that all sounds a bit over the top, you have to remember that I come from a bike background – and Honda have always produced the most competitive bike machinery. Yamaha and Suzuki have always been there racing, but Honda are the innovators, the company that comes up with the ideas that change sport. They produced a ground-breaking six-cylinder 250cc engine and turned out a four-stroke bike engine that revved to 24,000 rpm. They also made the monkey bike that got me started in motor-sport, so you could say I've been with Honda since the word go. My first-ever race was, in fact, on a Honda CB 500 in 1979 (when Ralf Schumacher was three years old).

The more I talked to Eddie, the more important the Honda aspect became to me. They are an amazing company,

and I knew the potential was there but that it was not being tapped completely. To somebody like me, who has an inquisitive mind, a competitive spirit and a sense of ambition, that was intriguing.

There were other bonuses too. I liked the fact that Jordan had a British sponsor to whom I would be a big asset. I knew I would be key to their marketing programmes so it would be important to them that the team did well and, because they were enthusiastic about having me on board, that gave me an added sense of security. On top of it all, there was the chance to go down in history as the first man to win a race behind the wheel of a Jordan car.

It was all too much to resist and, after months of toing and froing, my decision was made – I wanted to drive for Jordan, and I rang up Eddie to tell him the good news. After that, it was just a case of thrashing out a contract until we announced the marriage to the world.

I was happy with my decision. I had taken my time, looked at all the alternatives and come up with a logical answer. It was a good decision, one that I was sure would make me happy. It felt right.

"There was the chance to go down in history as the first man to win a race behind the wheel of a Jordan car."

No such thing as a free launch!

chapter two

EXPECTATION

Every season begins with each driver on the grid believing that things will go his way. It's part of the ritual. You look forward to a new team, or to new challenges and new rivalries. Even if you have worked out that you won't be challenging for the world championship, you normally set yourself goals. For me, from the moment I signed for Jordan, my goal was obvious. I wanted to be the first guy to win a Grand Prix in one of Eddie's cars, and I wanted to get back to running at the front.

Expectation, though, can sometimes turn out to be a bit of a burden, because it builds up steadily from the moment the previous season has come to an end. Once everybody had slapped Jacques on the back and had their moan about Michael's tactics in Jerez, there was not a lot else to talk about except what would happen in 1998. It didn't matter that there were precious few facts to work from.

There was one thing that the Press were intrigued about as the new season loomed and that was the identity of my new team-mate – Michael Schumacher's brother, Ralf.

It wasn't just the journalists who were interested in this particular confrontation, either. After all the battles I have had with Michael over the years, I was as unsure as anybody as to how my relationship with Ralf would pan out, even though I made a point of saying, from the start, that I didn't expect any problems. In fact, I wasn't sure what to expect. The only thing I did know was that Ralf had the reputation of being fast.

He had shown in 1997 that he could be quick and, going into his second season, he was regarded as a talented new boy, one of the best of the new generation. His one problem was in getting round the track for the first lap, where he had made a few mistakes and ended up in the gravel. That was the classic mistake for a young, keen driver to make, and, other than that, he looked good.

Ralf had somehow earned a reputation for arrogance and being a difficult person to get on with. He had obviously had some problems forming a decent working relationship with Giancarlo Fisichella over the course of the previous season, because the two of them had a public falling-out early on in the season and never got over that hurdle. Their problems looked to me to be the result of a couple of talented, quick drivers who were desperate to get the upper hand – but there were plenty of people saying that Ralf would give me a cool reception as well. It all made for an interesting brew, but I wanted to find out about my new team-mate for myself. Like everything else in Formula One, the important rule is to make up your own mind and follow your instincts. There are always hundreds of people telling you what to say, do and think, but you have to be your own man. As far as I was concerned, Ralf and I would start with a clean slate.

"Whatever I did, I found it hard to overlook the fact that my team-mate was a Schumacher."

I took the view that the Jordan drive would be a challenge and one of the first tasks was to establish myself in the team and with Ralf. Gerhard Berger's retirement at the end of the previous season meant that I would be the oldest driver in Formula One and here I was, pitting myself against the best of the young drivers. It was a risky move, but at least I would know how I was faring with getting older. If Ralf ended up blowing me away, the hint would be there that it was time to call it a day.

As challenges go, it was one that I liked. I was putting myself and my reputation on the line, but there was a strong possibility that we could do well and, if I could win the team's first race, there would be a place in the record books waiting for me. It all looked great, but, even after a few weeks, there was just one problem: whatever I did, I found it hard to overlook the fact that my team-mate was a Schumacher.

I considered the situation where I might be racing against Michael for track position or even challenging him for the lead. Ralf would be privy to confidential information about our car and race tactics, and that is not the sort of material that you want to see passed on to a rival. Michael and Ralf are brothers and I found it hard to stop worrying about him passing on our secrets. Would he do that? Would

Michael cajole information out of him? I didn't know and that worried me. In Spa, for example, I qualified ahead of Michael at a crucial point in the championship for him and that must have created a test of loyalties for Ralf – does he confer with his brother to help him towards the title, or does he withhold information from Michael to protect Jordan's chances?

On the face of it, I shouldn't have worried. Ralf was honest and fair as well as being fast. When he came up against Michael on the track, most notably in Austria, he battled him and didn't give an inch, which was great for everyone to see.

From the first time the car ran, it was clear we had problems to overcome. It wasn't so much the team's fault as a product of the circumstances they had found themselves in, but it was to hurt us enormously.

Our main problem was that, coming into the start of the year, we simply had not done enough testing. There had been some big changes, with Honda replacing Peugeot as the engine supplier, and that always causes some disruption. On top of that, there were also some unusual rule changes covering the design of the cars and the sort of tyres we would be using, and they made a big

A good pairing

difference to performance. On paper, we should have been able to cope as well as anybody, but Formula One has a habit of not following the script, and here was a prime example.

Honda could not supply us with their new engine until the start of the year and Peugeot, Jordan's former supplier, had taken all their engines off to Prost. It meant that Jordan had no way of running a car. That meant the team had no way of coming to grips with the implications of the new regulations. And that meant we had problems.

The 1998 regulation changes were bound to have a huge impact, so every team on the grid knew it was important to get ahead of the game. Williams had been testing since the previous summer with a narrow car fitted with grooved

tyres, which they could do because they would be using the same Renault engine from year to year. We didn't have that advantage so, while Villeneuve and Frentzen were getting in their preparations, we were left twiddling our thumbs.

In any case, I had been banned from doing any testing by Tom Walkinshaw. My contract with Arrows didn't expire until the end of the year, but I was hoping that he would tear it up as soon as the season was over – not a chance. Instead, he held me to the letter of the contract and told me that I was not allowed to do any work for Jordan. After I had finished the last race of the year in Jerez, which finished with my car breaking down again, I walked away from motor racing and didn't drive a racing car again until I got into a Jordan when they had their first test in February. In other words, I didn't do my first test with a narrow-track car fitted out with grooved tyres until a matter of weeks before the start of the season. That hurt me for sure.

I was sorry about the way things finished with Tom. The way he stopped me testing for Jordan was a bit of a snub, but it wasn't the whole story. Before any of that, he tried to infer that I had been sacked from his team, which was as far from the truth as it's possible to get.

I had done very little testing with Arrows over the course of the season, because so much was new in the team that it was hard enough getting the car from race to race without worrying about getting down to testing. Then, when it started running more reliably, we were in the period when I was thinking over my decision of whom I would drive for,

Rush hour
Montreal

and I was stopped from testing altogether. I was basically turning up for the races and nothing more. That's not enough driving to keep you in the groove so, by the time I got into a Jordan, I was out of practice.

With any skilled discipline, like golf or driving or playing a musical instrument, you have to practice, so I had been training, and go-karting. I had been left-foot braking in my road car because I thought it would be necessary this season. I was doing everything I could to try to stay sharp and that was why I was keen to do as much testing as possible to try to get on top of the new regulations and become familiar with the team. I needed to get myself back up to speed.

First of all, we had the long wait to get a car running on the track in 1998 trim. As soon as that happened, though, we came across a problem that I knew was going to rear its head – who gets to drive the car.

To be as successful as possible in Formula One, it can be an enormous advantage to be the number one driver in a team. That's a fact, not an opinion, and it's a fact that is reinforced each season. However, according to our contracts, Ralf and I held equal status within the team – what's known as having 'joint number one' drivers. That's all very well, but to win a championship in Formula One has often meant, in recent history, that you will have to beat Michael Schumacher, who very definitely holds number one status at Ferrari. My argument has always been that in order to level the playing field, any driver would stand a better chance without the added pressure of having to fend off a challenge from the other side of the garage.

There is another aspect, which Jan Lammers, the Le Mans-winning sports car driver, put quite well when he used the analogy of having one watch or two. With one watch you know what the time is, even if it's out by a few seconds, but with two watches, you're never sure which one to believe. It can be the same with drivers in a team.

If everything is focused on what one driver is trying to achieve, it is sometimes easier for the team to give that driver what he needs to enable him to give his best performance. When Mika Hakkinen and David Coulthard were fighting each other at every race for the first half of the season, Michael was there to make the most of the situation.

Compare that with the set-up at Ferrari, where Eddie Irvine will do whatever it takes to help Michael. At Suzuka last year, Eddie somehow managed to get himself into the lead of the race and then sacrificed his own chances so he could orchestrate things from the front in such a way that Michael ended up winning. That's the difference. While Mika and David were having to watch their backs, Michael didn't have to worry.

It's the same problem I had in 1995 when I was having to compete with David at a time when I should have been focusing entirely on trying to beat Michael. David could not win the championship, but he was still there at every race, trying to beat me or overtake me just at the time when I needed to concentrate on beating Schmacher. Talk about having to cope with the enemy within! I don't intend this to be construed as something personal against Michael – it is merely a tactical observation.

'Actually, Michael, he's not such a bad bloke.'

That's what I would have wanted and that is what I think would have given me the best chance of getting to the front again. If a team like Jordan could focus all their resources behind one quick driver, they could certainly turn out to be consistent challengers at the front of the field. Unfortunately, though, the number one status eluded me. I tried to persuade Eddie, but I had no luck. Ralf already had an agreement that guaranteed he would be a joint number one, and there was no way I could get around that.

The problem became evident at the start of the year when we did not have enough engines. That, in itself, was a bit of a surprise, and not something I expected from an organised, committed company like Honda. I had to share track time with Ralf, which meant that at a time when we needed desperately to get some testing done, I was compromised, he was compromised and the team was compromised. Neither of us had enough time and both of us were testing the same things. Frustration abounded.

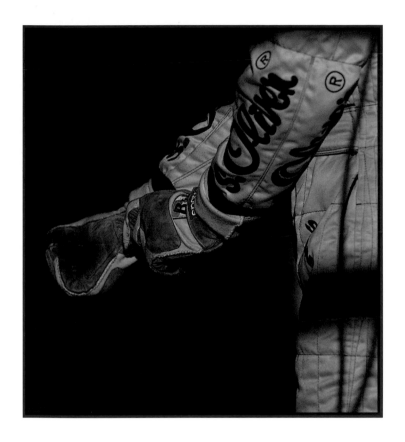

of the season. Up until then I was struggling to turn in the quality of performance that I knew I could, and should, be producing.

> "We realised we were a long way from where we wanted to be."

You can go for a month away from a car without losing too much, but I had not driven for more than three months, the longest period I had been away from a racing car since I started. In a racing car, you are dealing with tiny nuances and when you have been away, it is hard to put your finger on any one thing. You don't extend yourself as much, you think about it more instead of going by the seat of your pants. It is all mechanical instead of being flowing and instinctive.

I had already had a run on Bridgestone's grooved tyres while I was at Arrows, but that was my only experience of 1998 regulations. It gave me an inkling of what it would be like, but I didn't get a good idea until February, just a month before the first race. I had a lot of catching up to do and I was rusty.

It wasn't a case of forgetting how to drive or feeling badly out of shape, but you know when you are not right. There is a point when everything is working together and, whatever the state of the car, you know that you are pushing it, as well as yourself, to the limit. I didn't really get there until the San Marino Grand Prix in Imola, the fourth race

On top of that, the car didn't feel good, which was a lot to do with the tyres. The first time I drove it, my immediate reaction was that it was great to be back in a Formula One car. Then, after a bit, we looked at the lap times and saw where the other guys were and we realised that we were a long way from where we wanted to be. I was horrified.

There is an old saying in Formula One that if a car is quick out of the crate then it is going to be competitive all year, but this car certainly was not quick out of the crate. While there are an awful lot of things that can be done to a new car, the real indicator is how fast it is when it first runs. And ours simply was not fast enough.

There were so many problems with the way the car was handling that we had plenty of things to work on and we knew that if we could sort those out, then the car would go a lot faster. That gave us a chance to stand back and think about how we could improve the situation, and in times of crisis, you tend to look for any silver lining. The worst thing must be when you are happy with the handling, happy with yourself, and then you look at the times and see that the car is still miles off the pace. That is when you really need to worry.

I didn't like the way the car felt. It was too inconsistent and not very sensitive to changes in set-up and so I had to set off on the sensitive task of working to improve the situation. That's not an easy task for a new driver in a team and you have to tread carefully during the early days, building a sense of trust with the mechanics and engineers.

For years, they've been trying to beat you and now here you are, walking into their team and telling them what they've been doing wrong. When you're new to a team, it can be easier to make enemies than friends unless you are careful and considerate.

You have to build confidence in the team through what you do in the car. It's a catch-22 situation – until you take the car out and put in some really good lap times, they are not so sure about how much weight they should attach to your comments. The problem is that, unless they have confidence in you, how do you get them to change the car so you feel comfortable enough to put in those good times?

Fortunately, I have a good track record and it gave me a period of grace, but that only lasts a certain length of time before the questions start. It can go either way – you should hear some of the things I have heard mechanics say about a driver behind his back – but I was lucky. They wanted to hear what I had to say and they were sensible about it. We were able to get down to some work early on and that was vital because, even though I was cautious about the way I phrased it, it was obvious to me that there was something not right about the car.

The problem for me was that I didn't know how much was down to the tyre and design changes, and how much was down to me. I was experiencing a new mix of sensations, which was hard. I had to be careful what I said about the car, because for all I knew every other team was going through the same problems. When you add to all this the fact that I was a bit rusty, I was working hard to get the picture. That's why I needed as much testing as I could

get and that's why it was so frustrating when I found myself sitting and watching when I wanted to be behind the wheel.

Testing is how every driver and every team work out every problem. It's something I have always enjoyed and always been good at, and I didn't see any reason why that pattern should change at Jordan.

The way it works with me is that I become familiar with everything that goes on in the car and how it responds in different situations. There is only one way to do that, and it has to come down to the driver. It's no good for the engineer or even the designer to tell you how the car is going to behave, because you have to work it out for yourself, step by step. You become intimate with the car, but you can only do that by driving it over and over again.

Look at it this way – you can't get an orchestra to play a piece of music in one go. The conductor has to work out when the violins are too strong in one section, for example, or when the music should be slowed down a little and played a little more smoothly. It's like that with a racing

car. There are so many components that you have to learn how the various parts of each new car interact with each other. Only by making a lot of changes can you familiarise yourself with each component and the effect it has and, over a long period of time, you can work out which ones perform in what way. It is a laborious process, full of shifting sands, but it is the only way that works.

At the time, Jacques was complaining that the cars were feeling numb and I began to wonder if all the problems were down to the tyres. Then McLaren turned up with their car in Barcelona.

We did most of our testing in Barcelona, as did a lot of the other teams. We would watch our times and we would be okay and do a good time occasionally compared to, say, the Saubers. I was not comfortable though. We could do a good time at a certain moment in the day in certain conditions and that would look great on paper. But when you looked at the trends through the week, building up a picture and a pattern, I was less convinced. Formula One always comes back to the single, overwhelming need for people to be honest with themselves, rather than putting on a show, and if we were honest, we had to admit that a good few teams were looking quicker than us.

If that was bad enough, imagine our feelings when Mika Hakkinen turned up with his McLaren one day and, at about 5 p.m., goes out to do a few laps and is promptly 2.5 seconds per lap quicker than we had managed. He did five laps and then parked it and walked away, but that was

when the reality was brought home to us, like a punch in the gut. The prospect of trying to close that gap in performance seemed daunting. On top of that, I realised exactly what I had decided to turn my back on. That was the car I had been trying to get into and all my guesswork about its potential had turned out to be true. Emotionally, it was a little difficult to recover my equilibrium after that. I went back to my hotel room and just stared at the wall, gobsmacked. It was, all at once, impressive and enormously depressing, because it looked like Adrian had built a stonking car. I was secretly impressed, but I wasn't going to let anybody see that. Next day, it was back to work as if nothing had happened.

By now, of course, I had mentally committed myself to being at Jordan, but I didn't want to run the season being completely uncompetitive, because that can sap your morale. My experience had taught me that this was a situation that was shaping up to be tough and strenuous on everybody. The likelihood of us being able to win a race had been greatly diminished by the appearance of that McLaren, because you could be sure that Williams and Ferrari were also going to turn out decent cars.

Up until the first time I drove the car, I had been telling myself that we would be in the position to challenge and to win some races, but I couldn't help but reassess the situation in the light of Hakkinen's times. There was no use in pretending that everything would just sort itself out come the first race, so all we could do was come to terms with a new reality. But there was nothing to be gained by moping – I just had to get on with it and try to make things better.

Team working

And we did. We tested away, found some improvements and made progress, but before the first race we knew we were in the same boat as everybody else – a long way from beating McLaren. We put McLaren out of our minds, which is what most people did. We focused instead on looking at what was feasible, and that meant beating teams like Ferrari and Williams, who were also on Goodyear tyres. It was impossible to say what the Bridgestone advantage was, if anything, so you had to look at the teams who were on the same tyre as you, to give you a clue as to where you were.

Expectation sits on your shoulders all the time when you are driving a Grand Prix car; it's just that some people have more of it than others. I have sat on the grid in the last race of the year with the sole task of winning the world championship, and when you do that, you can't avoid the feeling that everybody is looking at you, willing you on, expecting you to fulfil their desires. Once you've put up with that, most other things seem a lot easier to take.

To some extent, I understand the fans' expectations because I have been there myself. I suspect I am unique

Eyes in the sky

as a driver because I spent most of my twenties being a fan of Grand Prix racing rather than ever taking part in it. I remember getting up at 3 a.m. in the hope that Nigel Mansell would become world champion on the other side of the world, and then watching him crash out with a puncture. I understand that tension and hope, and, since that night, I understand the disappointment as well.

I watched Nigel's first Grand Prix win from Paddock Hill bend at Brands Hatch. During every lap, I was holding on to the hope that it would work out right for him and that he would finally come home first and get to see that chequered flag. He was just ahead of Nelson Piquet and, because he had had a few moments in the past, we just stood there and hoped it would work out for him, that he would hold on. When he won, the feeling was as if I had taken my first breath of air since the start of the race. It was a sensation of complete elation.

It was the same feeling as when Arsenal won the FA Cup Final, a match I was delighted to be able to get to. I've supported Arsenal since I was a kid and it was great to be there to see them achieve something historic. Then, when I walked out of Wembley, a group of fans saw me and started chanting 'Damon is a Gunner'. They're right, so it was nice to be noticed!

Even before I won the championship, much had been expected of me and I have been lucky enough to have a lot of fans look out for me. It's flattering and, at times, it's a lot of fun, but this year I felt like saying to people, 'forget me for the moment because I am not in the frame. If I get up there, we'll all be happy, but . . .' I went to Monaco and met fans and they were asking, 'Are you going to win?' What could I say? I didn't want to say no and disillusion them, but at the same time I realised there was this great expectation that could not be satisfied at that moment. It was always going to take time with Jordan, but events like Canada just fuelled the situation and made it worse. A lot of fans tend to overlook the reasons behind a result. In Canada, I was running second because eight cars had, somehow or other, obliterated themselves.

Even in Canada, where you might imagine the support for Jacques and Michael would cut down on the Hill fans, I get great support. It's heart-warming and a valuable reminder that many fans still see our business as a sport.

To have that support is great, but the battle has to be fought by you alone. Once you get in the car, there is nobody else out there who can help you. Nobody can – not your friends, your family or your fans. You are on your own and, once you get over the nerves, it's a wonderful feeling to be in

"It is a wonderful feeling to be out there, in front of people cheering your name and waving their flags."

Fly the flag

England expects . . .

charge of the situation and in charge of your destiny. It is like the feeling you have when you have passed your driving test and you are allowed out there on your own, free of guidance, free to do what you want.

There are times when the sheer weight of support can still play its part though. Nigel used to tell people that driving in front of the Silverstone crowd was worth a second per lap to him, and although I think that's a bit of an exaggeration, it is a wonderful feeling to be out there, in front of people cheering your name and waving their flags. My first win at Silverstone was one of my greatest memories in motor racing, and I still remember so well the number of fans who urged me on through every lap.

People ask me why I've had all this support, and I've wondered too. I still don't know the answer. I try not to distance myself from people by putting up a façade, I try to be honest, and I think people appreciate that. If the simple act of being honest has endeared me to the fans, then it has brought me something that I did not expect. Looking back, though, I don't think my honesty has helped my career.

If you try to act in an honest, honourable, straightforward way, it affects the impression you give to the people who make the decisions, the people who assess you – team owners and journalists. Formula One is not about being pleasant and helpful. It's not about being decent and

honest. In this sport, it helps to be a hard-nosed bastard. Believe me, I can do that bit when I need to, but I don't necessarily enjoy it.

I think I have learnt to survive the hard way. I wore my heart on my sleeve in my early career and, while this may have shown my human side, it possibly gave the impression of a vulnerable character. When things did not work out in 1995, and I lost the title after giving everything I could, I was totally empty, drained of all my fight. I was a loser for all the world to see.

Nobody could have expected me to fight back from that. But I did. In fact, I won the last race of that year, in Adelaide. Nobody expected that, particularly Frank Williams and Patrick Head, who had already signed up my replacement.

You can't always have it both ways. Either you come across as being hard as nails, and maybe a little difficult to like, or you look human and perhaps expose your vulnerability to competitors and team bosses. Even if people like you, the general rule is: 'Everyone loves a winner.'

So the big question for 1998 was how we could do just that. With a world champion driver, a big sponsor in the shape of Benson & Hedges and a championship-winning engine supplier in Mugen-Honda, we had built up a high level of expectation. The trouble was that it was expectation built on a blancmange of a car.

The first race of the year is a little like the start of term – the same people, but in different places and uniforms. Ferrari and McLaren, after intentionally avoiding each other, are on the same track again. After all the months of planning and testing, now is when we find out where we stand, for better or worse. In some ways it can be a relief – until, as happened with us, you arrive in Melbourne to have your worst fears confirmed. As the two McLarens disappeared into the distance, there weren't too many smiles in the Jordan pit or, indeed, anywhere else.

The only thing to do at such times is to believe that things will improve, but there's no point just sitting there, with your fingers crossed, hoping that the car will get better. You have to find the reasons the car struggled in the first place and then get on and fix it. Knowing why one car is not as good as another is not always that straightforward.

As a driver, I see my job as directing the team to these shortcomings, suggesting new ideas and trying to keep people motivated when the prospects are looking bleak. Part of the way you do that is by expressing your own disappointment and pointing out the problems, whether they are in the team or the car, but that is when you can come in for criticism yourself. Just like the chassis, the engine or the tyres, if people are looking for a target, eventually they will remember that the driver is also part of the package.

Publicly, you can't afford to rise to the bait, but good racing drivers always analyse their races, looking for improvement. They consider the part played by every component, including themselves, and are the only ones who can really assess their own performance.

A driver's particular style is a totally individual thing. Somebody said that driving style is like handwriting, because the way you drive is an extension of your personality. People drive in subtly different ways from each other, in a style that they have crafted over the years. In most cases, this style has been worked out by the individual totally on his or her own. There are no David Leadbetters or Arsene Wengers in motorsport.

Because I started on motorbikes, I have a different style from most of the guys who came to motor racing through karting. You don't tackle corners aggressively on a bike; instead, you learn to blend braking, turning and accelerating. With that type of background, I developed into what I would describe as a smooth driver rather than somebody who throws his car around, but that doesn't mean that I am not as 'on the limit' as some of the others. All it actually means is that I explore the limit in my own way. I would liken my instinctive style to that of Alain Prost more than any other driver, although I sometimes change character to suit different circumstances.

Prost's style was so smooth that he made racing look easy. I won't forget Ayrton Senna watching the big screen showing Alain's hands on the wheel, via an 'in-kart camera', at the Elf Masters Championship in Paris. Ayrton watched him like a hawk, obviously impressed, for Prost was the master of understatement when it came to driving.

Other drivers, the ones who look as if they are having to work hard in the cockpit, fall into the 'wild' or 'spectacular' school, and that style also has its merits. Jean Alesi, Jacques Villeneuve, Mika Hakkinen and even, from time to time, Michael Schumacher, all tend to get out of shape every now and then. In the 1994 Benetton, Schumacher looked so busy in the cockpit, you could hardly believe that he could keep that up for a whole race. Those drivers throw their cars around, run wide on corners and put wheels off the road. In a race, it carries the risk of getting a puncture, but in qualifying, it can work to their advantage. And, of course, it does look spectacular.

A common problem in telling the difference between able and less able drivers is that what may look spectacular is not always fast. If a car is going sideways, then it's not going forward as much as it could be, because the tyres that hold us to the road can only do so much work – technically this is called a 'friction circle'.

"The art of driving is about balancing and juggling the different forces."

A tyre grips the road, and we try to find the limit of that grip. The driver knows when he's reaching the limit because, through the seat of his pants, his feet on the pedals and his hands on the steering wheel, he receives messages from the car and the tyres that he has to respond to.

Balance is vital. In braking, most of the load is taken through the front wheels, which is why we have bigger brakes at the front. In acceleration, all the load is taken through the rear wheels. The objective is to use to the full the combined braking, cornering and accelerating capabilities of the car – in other words, to find out how far you can drive around a corner without spinning off the track.

It might sound easy, and maybe it would be if we were driving on a billiard table surface with a constant-radius corner and a perfectly balanced car, but that never happens. Instead, the art of driving is about balancing and juggling the different forces, and being sensitive to those four small patches of tyre that connect you to the track. Differences in style come down largely to the ways in which drivers cope with that juggling act.

You can observe this most closely in the way a car goes into a corner. Everything starts from that vital point in the same way that everything follows on from the backswing in golf. How hard a driver hits the brakes as he comes to a corner has an enormous effect on how balanced the car is on the entry to a corner. Some drivers have a very aggressive initial braking, like Alesi, and this puts the whole bias towards the front of the car, so that the back end becomes light and difficult to control. Luckily for him, Jean's great strength lies in his ability to control just that sort of

Me in the green T-shirt eyeing up the master, Monaco 1988

problem. Hakkinen, too, turns in very late and hard, rather like a rally driver.

By contrast, when I have the car set up well, I require small adjustments on the wheel, and my brake wear and fuel consumption are normally much lower than my team-mate's – Prost was the only exception. Giancarlo Fisichella, the

Benetton driver, is another in the same camp, relying on finding as smooth a line as he can through the corners. I believe this is the most efficient way but, as I say, it's all a matter of opinion.

There isn't a right way and a wrong way. Jean has his style and I have mine, and we both try to do our best. Jacques

Improvisation Alesi style

Villeneuve drives in his own particular style and it won him a world championship in 1997. I tend to think that all those moments when he puts two of his wheels on the grass cost him more time than they gain, but Jacques wouldn't be the same driver if he wasn't so keen on finding 'the edge'. It's great entertainment and, even if it's not my style, I would certainly pay to watch Villeneuve driving when he's got a head of steam up.

My father, in one of his first race meetings, was black-flagged for spinning seven times and he was brought in to the pits and told to calm down. His reply was: 'How can I take the car to the limit if I don't know where it is?' In a way, he was right – you have to go beyond the limit in order to know where it is. Jacques thinks like that as well; the difference is that he is not afraid to include an accident just to be totally sure.

As a breed, most drivers are stubborn. If the engineer sits down with his driver and tells him to do something else, a lot of guys will struggle against acting on that advice. It's to do with an ingrained sense of being comfortable with one way of driving, rather than malice or arrogance. Essentially, their style is their style and, like handwriting, it is very hard to change. There are odd bits that they might pick up, but most drivers can only drive one way. Indeed, many of us don't want to change something that we feel works well enough, and there's something to be said for that approach too.

A handful of drivers will try to adapt and learn – the sort who strive to improve their skills – and historically, the champions come from that select band. Niki Lauda, for example, used his intelligence to make himself the best that he could be. He was always very talented, but he also taught himself how to perform in every situation.

Twilight zone – Jacques loses control of the horizontal

Learning a new driving technique at home

I have always been keen to try out new ideas, but it's not easy to adapt and it gets more difficult the longer you drive. For a few years, I tried left-foot braking, a karting technique that a lot of young Grand Prix drivers now use so they do not have to transfer their right foot from the throttle to the brake and back again throughout the race. It also means you can trim the balance of the car by braking and accelerating at the same time and, if you get it right, it's a way of driving that can probably serve you quite well.

The trouble is that I grew up driving a different way, using my right foot on the brake, just as you do in a road car, and my left foot is not as sensitive to braking as my right. I might get there if I spent a year practising the technique in races, but I would lose a lot of time over that year and it's hardly worthwhile. If I was twenty-four years old, I would do it, but as I'm a little older than that, I think I will stick with my old friend, the right foot.

Generally, though, I am very willing to adapt my style. If the data says I should be doing something new, then I will give it a go. It might suggest that there is another line through a corner or a way of turning in that will give me a better time, so I'm happy to go out and put the idea into action. If it works, then it could mean another couple of places on the grid. If it doesn't, then you can scrub it off the list and look for the next bright idea.

In the wet, you're forced to make changes, both to the set-up of the car and to your driving style, whoever you are. When rain comes down, turning the racetrack into something of an ice-rink, a driver has to be more aware than ever of that balancing act between cornering, braking and accelerating.

For me, it still comes back to the lessons I picked up while riding bikes. You need a lot of nerve to lean a bike over and put the power down through a corner when it is pouring with rain, and you become very alert to the level of grip that you have. Funnily enough, the best practice came while I was a despatch rider, charging through London in all conditions. There are some particular roads, such as Belgrave Square, that get very slippery in the wet, so I used those opportunities to learn to powerslide the rear wheel and get a bit crossed-up. It was very good training and the best way to brighten up a dull day.

In the wet, you can play with the car and have fun, balancing it with the throttle and letting the wheels slide on purpose. You have to concentrate much harder because a curve that barely merited a thought when it was dry becomes a corner and the straights that were previously flat-out blasts become skid-pans. On a wet track, you can't simply thump your foot down on the gas and start thinking about the next corner because, with the amount of power the cars

"If the data says I should be doing something new, then I will give it a go."

have, you could find yourself spinning like a top before you ever get there.

You have more opportunities to pick different racing lines in the wet. The game becomes dominated by the need to find a section of the track that will let your car grip the surface as hard as possible, and it's a different challenge at every circuit. At some places, the usual racing line is marked with streaks of oil and rubber that get treacherously slippy in the rain, so at those circuits it's better to look for an alternative. At other places, where the track offers more grip, the normal line can still be the best solution.

A tactical decision such as that comes down to a driver's experience and his ability to size up a situation. The good guys will be thinking all the time about looking for grip, and they might change their line on every lap. In bad weather, those are the drivers to look out for – the guys who are thinking all the time and looking for the advantage.

Wet weather racing has a drama of its own, because it tends to come down to a few crucial decisions. The first one presents itself if it starts to rain while you are on dry tyres. Do you wait to see if it eases off? Do you come in early and try to steal an advantage, or do you leave it late to change? After all, if you change on to wet tyres and the weather improves, you'll have to make another pit-stop to change back again, wasting crucial time.

**Wet seat of the
pants driving**

Another crucial decision must be made when there is so much rain that everybody has to slow down a lot. You don't want to reduce your own speed, because that goes against a racer's instinct, but something inside you says, 'this is crazy – you can't drive flat out in these conditions'. That moment is when you have to negotiate with yourself and come up with a compromise: fast enough to race, slow enough to keep the car under control.

Inside the car, you're soaked. Imagine sitting in a chair with a wind machine blasting you and somebody hosing you down for two hours, and that will give you an idea of what it is like to race in the rain. If it's a hot day, then the conditions are not so bad, because the rain cools you down and can make you feel quite fresh, but there are not many hot rainy days. Usually it's cold, so you end the race shivering and feeling like a lump of ice, which makes it difficult to jump when you're on the podium.

There are advantages to wet weather racing, though. It can reward the better drivers, and it gives you a chance to play with your tactics. It is also easier to overtake in the wet, so long as you can see through the spray.

The level of grip offered by the car is amazing. Because of the amount of downforce holding you to the track, you can go through deep puddles flat out and still come out the other side in a straight line, feeling no more than a deceleration as the car pushes away the water. Water is 800 times more dense than air, so we go slower on the straights in the rain as a result of this 'boating effect'. On

Examining the conditions

61

other occasions, though, you suddenly have no grip and you feel the car lift off the road or start changing direction. All you can do is react with the steering wheel and the throttle, and hope for the best. It's interesting . . .

In conditions like that, it is vital to have a good set-up on your car so that it's balanced and responsive. A driver needs to feel comfortable that he can control his car in corners and get as much speed as possible on the straights, and, whatever the conditions, if he's good at that aspect of the sport, he can hold a considerable advantage over the field.

"The work done in those long test sessions is critical to success."

It is vital to communicate and work with the engineers. Drivers don't have to understand the physics and the engineering of their car, but it can help the engineers to come up with solutions more quickly if the driver can make suggestions, such as adjusting the roll bar or dampers, and talk accurately about the sensations he experienced while driving. If he simply leaps out of a car without giving any guidance, then he leaves a lot of holes for the team to fill in with educated guesswork.

Despite all the information we get from the telemetry and the onboard computers, it is still necessary for the driver to communicate exactly what it is about the car that is holding him back, and some drivers are better at this sort of dialogue than others. The good ones can go to a test

session and really make the most of the time, trying out new ideas and improving the machinery. The bad ones just drive around in circles.

The work done in those long test sessions is critical to success in Formula One. By pounding the car for lap after lap, you can look for improvements and hopefully come up with the tweaks you need to claw back the missing time. The problem, of course, is that every other team is also testing, trying out their own ideas and searching for ways to improve their cars. It's a battle away from the races, but it has a direct bearing on what happens during a Grand Prix. A team that uses its testing time well is normally a team that gets stronger all through the year.

I don't have the skills to design and you won't ever see me telling designers how to do their job, but I can be their eyes in the car. I can tell them what happens in their car when it is being driven hard, how it performs and how it can perform better. I tell them how it behaves through certain corners, whether it's well balanced or being held back by peculiarities in the suspension or in the aerodynamics. They have plenty of information sent back to them by computer links as well, but the driver's input can make the difference. The facts on the computer show what the car is doing in terms of speed, acceleration, power and so on, but it is the driver's responsibility to say if he can drive it or not. That is the point when a good designer or engineer comes into his own.

If there was one thing that Tom Walkinshaw did that might have persuaded me to stay at Arrows, it was to sign up John Barnard to design the cars and do the job of

Spray, OK if you're in front

Newey knows, but leaves me guessing

technical director. John is a man full of innovative ideas and is willing to try them out. I got on very well with him and he made a healthy difference to the team. It was largely thanks to him that the car ran so well in Hungary last year, because his ideas helped us to have the car set up perfectly for the race and, with a bit more luck, we would have won. John's talent was one of the main strings to the Arrows bow, but without a powerful engine there was not a lot that even he could do for the team in 1998.

There are some very talented people in Formula One working on the technical side and their ability can make the difference between winning and losing. John is one;

another is Adrian Newey, the man whose designs helped McLaren start the season with such a clear advantage.

I have known Adrian since I started out in Formula One. He produced his first car for Williams in the year that I took over the role of team test driver, so I got a close-up look at his skill early on.

I started off my testing career with a single test behind the wheel of an FW13 car, which had been designed by Patrick Head, the team's technical director. After that, I moved on to the FW14, which was Adrian's design. As test driver, it was my job to work closely with the designer, telling

64

The innovative John Barnard

him how the car was performing out on the track. From the very beginning, we got on well and worked as a team.

I was very interested in learning about Formula One cars and Adrian helped me enormously. Then, in 1996, he played a big part in helping me to win the world championship, not only by designing the car, but also by giving me advice on how to prepare it for each Grand Prix.

My interest in Formula One is heavily biased towards the technical side and I am intrigued by people like Adrian and John Barnard, people who are interested, above all, in finding answers to difficult questions. I have that curiosity, but I am afraid that I have none of the qualifications, except a Physics O-level, which simply isn't enough nowadays.

The sort of engineers who are succeeding in Formula One car design today are people like Adrian and a whole new breed of highly qualified specialist aerodynamicists. Eddie Jordan made a smart move by enlisting the services of the highly rated Mike Gascoyne later in the season, after we realised that our car needed some serious attention in that area. Mike has a double first in fluid dynamics from Southampton University, which makes my O-level look a bit puny.

My father had a love of technology and machinery, and that fascination was passed on to me from my earliest days. It was one of those interests that we shared and I took to avidly. Like most children, I used to like making things. I made models and spent a lot of my time finding

Advice from Patrick Head at my first Formula One test with Williams

out how things worked by taking them apart. I loved to strip down cars and bikes and leave them like that. Rebuilding was a talent that I only acquired much later, and resulted in some very messy situations early on.

During my first years of racing motorbikes, I stupidly didn't want anybody to help me, so I did all the work myself. I knew what to do if the bike was not running well, how to prepare and adapt it and to make sure that if a problem came up, I knew how to solve it. I made plenty of mistakes along the way, but I was always learning and fiddling with the machinery, feeling a tremendous sense of satisfaction when I made a change that turned out to have a good effect. I also got to know the feeling of frustration that comes from mechanical failure, and I have never got over that.

A few years ago, I worked with Adrian and Patrick Head, the Williams technical director, on what were known as the active-era cars. It was all about cutting-edge technology and the most sophisticated machinery that motor racing had ever known, with suspensions that controlled the height of the car as you went round corners and traction control systems that ensured your wheels never spun while you were accelerating. We were scratching the surface of what was technologically possible at the time. They were all new and different ideas and concepts, and we were having a good time.

Then, as soon as they had come, active cars were banned. For those of us who had taken an interest in the way the cars were being developed, it was a disappointment, but not nearly as much as it was for the poor guys, like Frank

Williams and Ron Dennis, who had forked out millions to develop the systems. Some of the technical developments we had been working on then would have taken us down an entirely new design route because they were so innovative and exciting. Up until then, the limitations on how we worked and even how we thought had been fairly strict, but all of a sudden, there was a world of computer-controlled suspensions and differentials, ideas that were completely new and that forced us to open our imaginations to what could be achieved.

For me, it was fascinating. It was truly a wild ride in an F1 car. I cherish the memory of driving the Williams active car around Estoril in winter testing in 1992 with traction control, anti-lock brakes, large qualifying tyres that had no grooves and a 3.5-litre engine. It was awesome, and more.

It must be so odd for people such as Adrian and Patrick to design these wonderful cars but never know what they are like to drive. I know they get a sense of satisfaction from seeing them being driven hard and used properly, but they wouldn't be human if, once in a while, they didn't wonder what it's really like to be inside the cockpit for a flat-out lap. Instead, they have to put up with people like me coming back into the garage and complaining that 'it's not quite right'.

After our problems in Australia, my new colleagues at Jordan were hearing plenty of that from me. I didn't throw my toys out of the pram, but I was not a happy camper, either – which is technical speak for trying to keep calm after a disappointing eighth place 12,000 miles from home.

Early test shot at Silverstone

The start of the San Marino Grand Prix did nothing to suggest our luck was improving. I had a collision with Alex Wurz at the first corner and damaged the front wing of my car, leaving me to crawl back to the pits. By the time I came out again, I was in nineteenth place and the rest of the pack had disappeared into the distance.

It was not a pretty sight. We had no points from the first three races and here I was, almost last after one lap. From there, things could only get better and, to my pleasant surprise, they did. I started moving up through the field and ended up improving my position by eleven places. Then, while I was standing eighth, with an eye on picking up a point, the car broke down.

It was frustrating, but it proved one thing – it was a fighting recovery and underlined my determination to give my best, whatever the circumstances. I want to do well, to win and battle. The experience of driving is great, but that's not what racing is all about. If the sport did not have a competitive element to it, I wouldn't find it nearly as stimulating.

It is not enough to drive around a circuit purely for the hell of it. What keeps me going back to motor racing again and again is the competition – the opportunity for most of the world's best drivers to pitch themselves against one another. You are under enormous pressure to perform and, under those circumstances, you get a good idea of how your skills stack up against the rest of the field.

I look at my tally of results, the number of races I have won and the pole positions I have held, and I tot them up in the same way an actor might look at the awards he has been given. They are my measure of achievement, a record of what I have done in Formula One, and I'm proud of them.

You cannot trade them in and they cannot be taken away from you. They are there for the record books and, when I stop driving, I will be able to look back at those results as a testament to all the hard work that went into climbing to the top. The question is, though, what pushed me to climb that high in the first place?

I have tried to understand the source of my motivation and ambition, because perhaps it holds the secret to getting the best out of oneself. There is a heavy cost to being a Grand Prix driver – the risks you face while driving and the family and social life that you miss out on – and I want to know why I have been so willing to meet that cost.

Whatever the root cause might be, it manifests itself in my competitive drive. Whatever it is that I'm doing, I have to set new targets and challenges to fire my motivation. There has to be something to aim for to keep me interested, some ambition has to be fulfilled – but the question I always ask myself is why? What is this bug that forces me to keep on pushing myself? Is it something particular in my make-up, or is it just human nature?

For a while, I was worried that I was trying to overcome a deep-rooted dissatisfaction with myself and needed to achieve something to be proud of. My father was a world-famous personality so, growing up, I felt strongly that I had to go into the world and establish myself on my own terms. I dreaded the thought of being seen as someone who has had success handed to him on a plate.

> "To a great extent, I became a racing driver despite, rather than because of, my father's reputation."

Ironically, despite all the accusations that I have been helped in my career because of my name, it would actually have been much easier to have walked away from racing at the very start, and avoided all the obvious comparisons. I considered this, but the bottom line is that I enjoy racing and I enjoy going fast. If I had not been a racing driver, then I would have been spiting myself just for the sake of avoiding comparison and I was not prepared to do that. To a great extent, I became a racing driver despite, rather than because of, my father's reputation.

It still took me time to understand and deal with his legacy, but eventually I realised that there was nothing I could do about what other people thought or remembered. I never fought against my father's performances and, regardless of the respect I still have for him, his achievements are not relevant to mine. I have my own problems and challenges, and there is nothing to be gained by trying to emulate the way he handled himself. We are different people and, despite all the questions about my father that have been put to me over the years, I made my own way in life and set goals for myself. Just like him, I have had ups and downs, and have always dealt with them as best I could.

You can't tackle motor racing in a half-hearted fashion. It's a sport that requires a lot of effort, through training and stress, and there has to be a pot of gold lurking at the end of the rainbow to push you on, a meaningful reward that will make all the effort worthwhile.

For many drivers, the source of the ambition to become world champion does not bear further analysis. Like Everest, it's just there – 'I'm a driver, I want to get to the top to prove that I'm the best.' Fine. It would be great if a driver was declared the best upon becoming champion, but that doesn't happen automatically. I remember watching a television interview with Jacques Villeneuve the morning after he had won the title in 1997. The interviewer kicked off straight away with 'This doesn't mean much, does it, because you had the best car?'

Winning the championship is merely a step on the way to being regarded as the best. If winning is the goal because it is a rare experience, then that is reason enough, but you have to realise that it's not a feeling that will last for ever. Unlike a trophy, you won't be able to hang on to that emotion, or hold the attention of the world for your achievement indefinitely, but it's nice to have had it once!

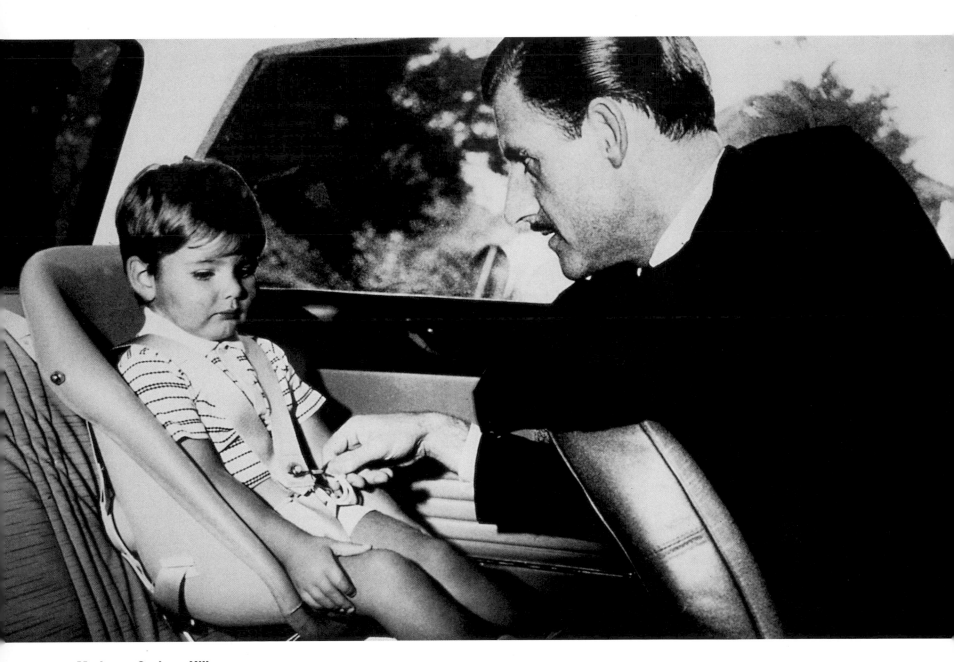

My hero, Graham Hill

Only a game? . . . with my sisters Brigette and Samantha

Of course, the experience is addictive and draws us all back for another hit, to relive that moment, to get that high again, but sooner or later it will slip beyond each driver's capabilities as surely as winter follows summer. Then, it's just a dream, as it was in the beginning, with only a few photographs to help convince you that it was real. I don't display any of my trophies or hang pictures of my greatest moments in my house, because I feel that as long as I'm still competing, whatever I have done in the past is irrelevant to the present and I don't want to have to keep reminding myself or my guests about how brilliant I used to be. I'm not that sad, yet.

Grand Prix literally means 'Big Prize', but, in truth, there is no actual big prize for winning in Formula One, at least not in the way that most of us would expect. It's not like the Indianapolis 500, for instance, where the winner is not even out of his car before the giant-sized 'check' is presented to him, so that all the viewers can make the connection between winning and reward.

In Formula One, the system is a little more complex, but it does ultimately follow that the better you do on the track, the better you can potentially do off it. Rather than there being an automatic return, there will have to be a

Trying not to lose sight of our goal

negotiation with the team, the sponsor or whomever. It makes for an interesting relationship between the driver and the team boss, because there always seems to be a disparity between how each party views the reasons for their mutual success.

However, if a driver devotes the best years of his life to racing a car, he had better be a good negotiator or not care about the money. I tend to think it is prudent to earn as much as possible during my career, since I'm poorly qualified to do much else once I've retired from Formula One racing.

While money may be an objective, it is not necessarily a motivating factor. I was offered a deal once which was aimed at motivating me to win by linking payment directly and solely to race wins. Since I do not race to win money, I felt that, by accepting such a deal, I would have confirmed the team's wrong impression of the source of my motivation. Winning and money are totally separate issues, but it's hard to convince set commercial minds of that fact.

Even so, after a point, greater financial reward becomes an abstraction. I have met enough rich men who would have given anything to have stood on the top of the podium if only money could buy that. And I have also seen plenty of rich racing drivers who looked like they had nothing left to live for after a poor result. Not winning hurts.

Fame can lure us to do things we might otherwise not consider, but fame is a two-faced friend. I don't mind having my picture all over the place for having done something I'm proud of, but I was once presented to the world as the 'Prat' after knocking off Schumacher at Silverstone in 1995. To change that particular perception can certainly be a motivation.

Perhaps I would be better off not analysing why I want to win. Then again, it can be no bad thing to think through the motivating factors before embarking on a perilous and emotionally stressful journey. Imagine if you won the title, having made all those sacrifices, and found yourself un-satisfied and disappointed. The sense of anti-climax would be enormous.

Quite often, in fact, it is the struggle itself that is the most enjoyable part of any competition. That is what you have to look back on and, by seeing the efforts you had to make, the end result appears all the more valuable. If a driver's first title is a walkover, he might wonder whether it is worth all the effort; if he has to fight to the last race, he feels like a true champion.

When you get into Formula One, your first target is to win a race. If you're lucky enough to do that, and most people

Rowing up that hill in the gym at home

'You've been champion for five minutes – what does it feel like?'

aren't, then you have give yourself new targets. If you've won one race, you've got to win another. Maybe you've got to aim to win two in a row, or pick up a certain number of victories in a season. Most of all, though, you want to go for the world championship.

What happens if you manage that feat is a more difficult question. You've achieved the ultimate challenge and, although the obvious thing is to try to repeat that success, you start to ask yourself what's next. Going for another title is not as appealing a proposition as it sounds, because winning one championship is a huge mental and physical struggle. At the end of the season, you are

exhausted in every way and the last thing that the rational part of your mind wants you to do is put yourself through that amount of strain all over again.

It was two full days after winning my world championship in 1996 that I finally woke up and realised what I had done. It was almost as if a voice in my head suddenly said, 'It's okay, Damon, you can have a cup of tea now and put your feet up.' For the previous forty-eight hours, my life had been chaos of press interviews and appearances. Although I was talking about the title, I didn't have any time to think about it for myself. It was only when I had some peace and quiet that the whole thing sunk in.

Point made . . . sixth place at Silverstone 1997

What I had was a feeling of relief that lasted for a good couple of months, a feeling of satisfaction and contentment that it had turned out all right in the end. At that point, all the struggles, pain and cost were worth it. I had set out to do something and, to my immense delight, I had done it.

Having won that world championship, I looked at my career in a fresh way. Chasing the championship had provided me with ambition and motivation for most of my career, but now that focus had changed. I found myself questioning my future and wondering whether I should carry on accepting the risks of driving a racing car now that I had achieved my ambition.

After all, it looked like I was going back to square one. Joining Arrows was not going to give me the chance to retain my title and the general opinion was that, at thirty-six, I had won my one and only world championship and, quite

Hail the conquering hero

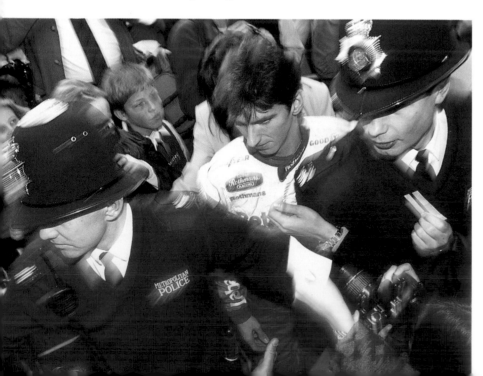

possibly, my last Grand Prix. It wasn't a view that I liked to hear, but I would have had difficulty arguing against it.

I considered retiring after the disappointment of losing my Williams seat, but I was not prepared to throw away all my experience and abilities by giving up, even if I was champion. I felt I had more to put into the sport and I didn't want to sit at home, watching enviously from the sidelines. I made the firm decision to carry on, and if that meant trying to take Arrows by the scruff of the neck for a year, then so be it.

It was frustrating though. I had learnt so much and, having crossed the Rubicon by winning a title, I knew that if I ever got the opportunity again, things would be a lot easier. Now I knew how to win a title and what the mistakes were, but I was in a car that couldn't offer me the same opportunities. The golden rule is to get yourself in a competitive team and, in 1997, it looked as if I had broken that rule.

The Arrows gave me no chance of retaining my title, so I had to find a new challenge to keep me fired up for the season. Searching for motivation can be a problem, but in my circumstances I didn't have to look far. In fact, all I had to do was listen to my critics.

One of the biggest accusations that was thrown my way after winning the title was the tired old cliché that I only won races because I was in the best car. I knew in my heart that was not the case, but I felt it would be nice to turn things around to prove finally that I was a driver who had more ability than I had been given credit for. I was given that chance by Arrows. If I could push their car nearer

Fast – but not fast enough, Arrows 1997

to the front than anybody else had done, then I could prove to the world that, beyond everything else, I was a driver who deserved to be called world champion – someone who really could race. And that is what I set out to do.

There were some very high moments, such as taking the lead in Hungary and almost taking pole position for the last race of the year in Jerez, but there were some low times as well. The car was not good, and that created problems for everybody, including me. If you are being paid as a sportsman and things are not going well, then you are going to get flak from all directions. Nobody likes to see someone being paid a lot of money and then apparently not delivering, but, then again, nobody was more disappointed than me about the car's shortcomings. I am in Formula One because I get a buzz out of racing and improving a car. Going backwards is not one of my ambitions. During my season with Arrows, Tom Walkinshaw

took the opportunity of the British Grand Prix, with its high profile in the media, to claim that I had not been pulling my weight in the team. He said I had lost some of my motivation and that I was not trying hard enough. When I heard that, I was furious.

An accusation like that does nothing to motivate me to perform better. It's the sort of soundbite that flies around and then, before you know it, there is a chorus of people dutifully following the theme. It was hardly my fault if I was being paid a lot of money to drive a car that was not very good. Having a good tactical brain doesn't come into play very much when you are eighth and going backwards, after all. Instead, what tends to come out is the frustration felt by everybody seeing their investment in time and money being wasted.

Criticism like Tom's tells you one thing above all else – the boss is fed up about his team's lack of success. When I went out later that weekend and scored a point in front of the Silverstone crowd, the suggestion was that my drive was inspired by criticism. That couldn't be further from the truth. Just because there is an upturn in performance after a driver is slated publicly, it doesn't mean the two things go together, and in this case it didn't follow at all. It is in my nature to want to succeed and put everything I have into my driving. I wouldn't have made it to Formula One if that were not the case and that was why I scored a point

that day for Arrows and for Tom. It had nothing to do with the comments he had thrown in my direction, and everything to do with putting a hell of a lot of effort into a race and getting a bit lucky with a few non-finishers in front.

Racing hard is something that must be instinctive to me. From the very first seconds that I rode a motorbike as a child, I knew it was the best thing I had ever done and I have never lost that sense of excitement and determination. There is a common link between that childhood experience and my racing since – exhilaration through acceleration. That simple formula has served me for more than three decades.

I skied for the first time when I was five or six and loved it, and I rode that bike when I was ten. Even then, I didn't want to pootle round on it. I wanted to go fast.

I don't think my love of speed came from being in the Hill household, because I had no ambition at all to be a racing driver. Cars did not appeal to me at all, whereas bikes were my fascination.

On a motorbike, you became a part of the machine. There is a spiritual dimension to a bike. The angle of lean makes the experience closer to flying than driving a car, which works in a flat plane. On a bike, every movement of your body has an effect – the bike moves with you, so in some

"It is in my nature to want to succeed and put everything I have into my driving."

ways you feel as if the machinery is an extension of yourself. It is a very harmonious experience.

I started to race regularly when I was nineteen years old. I worked as a builder during the week and that provided enough money for me to buy my first bike and get on a track. I owned an old van and, first thing on Saturday morning, I would put the bike into the back of the van and go off racing. It meant everything to me.

I had a vision of myself winning, but there was one major problem: I simply did not know how to do it. All that kept me going was a bloody-minded determination that I was not going to accept defeat, and I took that attitude into

everything I did. Whether it was not having the money I needed or the van breaking down on the way to the circuit, I saw every problem as a personal challenge that I had to overcome.

I refused help because I wanted to succeed for myself, but I had entered national races where the standard of racing was too high for a solitary rookie. All I had was my obsession, not just with racing, but with the idea of shaping my own destiny and discovering things for myself.

In my first race, I turned up on an out-of-date road bike, a second-hand Honda CB500 bought from Elite Motors in Tooting that was not suitable for racing in any way. I didn't

Communication breakdown with Tom Walkinshaw

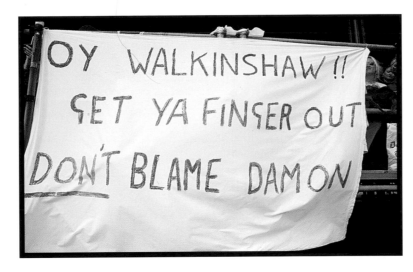

**My mother
took it badly**

tune it or change the tyres, but simply taped up the lights and charged out on to the track as fast as I could.

In my mind, I was instantly about to become a Barry Sheene. I thought my talent would surpass everything and imagined, terribly naïvely, that the machinery was not important. I thought that if I was good enough, I would win on any bike I cared to use and, lumbered with that attitude, I spent three years struggling along at the back of the field. I couldn't even start my bike properly, so at every race I was still trying to get going while the rest of the field were streaming around the first corner. I was hardly going to win this way, but I stupidly thought that determination would be enough.

However brave a face I put on the situation, it was a desperate disappointment and I nearly made the decision to stop racing. My career up until then had been a dismal, frustrating failure, but I did not want to give up. Things had to change, though, so I made the decision to move down

a level or two and take a long look at what I was doing. It was the first good move I made, because finally I was waking up to the fact that you do not turn up and become world champion the next day. You have to learn your craft and channel your efforts in the right direction. That's as good a lesson for a racer to learn today as it was sixteen years ago.

I changed the carburettors and concentrated on getting the bike to start with the first push. I also began to race at Brands Hatch every weekend, which made me a master of both that circuit and the South Circular Road. I thought a lot more about the skills involved, and I even began talking to some of the other people in the sport after years of keeping to myself. All of a sudden, I became a winner.

To this day, the first win I had remains one of the most satisfying experiences of my career. It was in 1983, three years after my first race, and it felt wonderful.

The start of it all at Donnington, 1980

I won the race by a long way. Exactly how far, I will never know, because I didn't dare to look back from the moment I got into the lead until I saw the chequered flag, fearful that somebody was about to overtake me. When I crossed the finishing line, the overwhelming feeling was of disbelief, because I had tried so hard to win for all those years and suddenly I had cracked it. I just didn't really know why.

After that first victory, I started to win all the time. Suddenly I felt unbeatable. I had Brands Hatch sussed and, whatever the level of competition, I always seemed to win there.

Just as they were to do after my Formula One title many years later, the sceptics suggested that I was winning because I had better machinery. Then, at one race, the gearbox broke on my bike and I couldn't use it. John Webb, then the circuit owner, lent me some money from the cash till and told me to go out into the paddock, find somebody

with a similar bike to mine, and hire it. So I did, and even though the tyres were different from the ones I was used to, which worried me a little, I won the race. There was no let-up in my performance, so everybody could see that my success was down to me, not the bike. More importantly, *I* could see that maybe it was me and not the bike.

Buoyed up by my new-found success, I started to consider the long-term prospects of being a motorbike racer, and realised they were not good. Not many British riders made much money, and very few had long careers. The thought hit me that if I wanted to race for a living, then I probably shouldn't do it on bikes. For the first time in my life, I started thinking about trying out cars instead.

Because of my father, I knew people in the motor racing world and I was aware that there were drivers, some of them in their fifties, who made good money from their

Still got the bug in 1998, on a 1958 Manx Norton

Barry Sheene, my boyhood hero, takes my threats seriously, Goodwood 1998

Prelude to F1 – leading F3000, Monza 1990

**Formula Ford
championship 1985**

racing. The idea of having a steady income and racing fast cars to boot began to look better and better. The more I considered it, the more cars began to take on a whole new attraction. If you want your racing to be serious, it has to be a full-time profession and motor racing seemed to offer that. It was a pragmatic career change.

No matter that the vehicle was now different, my desire to succeed was simply transposed to my career as a racing driver and my motivation was to win and get paid for it. I did not expect to get rich, but I did not want to have to race part-time and earn an income on the side. Quite soon I became as single-minded and obsessive about car racing as I had been about bikes.

The racing was competitive and it was motorsport so, in that sense, there was not a lot of difference between cars and bikes. The trouble was that, until then, I had not taken the slightest bit of interest in motor racing. I was working as a despatch rider and racing bikes in my spare time, and that didn't leave me any time to spend watching cars. I knew about the history of the sport, of course, but I was

not a regular viewer of Grands Prix. That had to change. From the moment I decided to switch to cars, I started to watch Formula One all the time. I regarded that as one of the duties of my new job.

When you have raced a racing bike, though, you cannot love a Formula Ford car, and that was my entry level. The first time I ever drove a car that had anything like the power-to-weight ratio and grip of a 350 Yamaha racing bike was in Formula 3000, the rung below Formula One. Up until then, the cars were all underpowered and over-gripped. They were still exciting, and the competition was good, but that feeling of exhilaration that you get from a bike was not there.

The only thing that comes close to the feeling of a racing bike is a Formula One car. There is nothing superfluous about a racing bike, nothing that does not add to the performance. Other car formulae are designed to be restrictive, which makes them a little crude, but Formula One cars use high-tech materials that take the sport to the nth degree. It is nearly as good as we can achieve.

Well, it's a start . . . Brabham 1992

badly affected. You can't fight and that means you cannot do what you are being paid to do, because you are handicapped by the equipment.

It would be no good for England to play Michael Owen in goal because he is the guy who can score goals, and he isn't going to do it from there. He would get pretty fed up if he had to play a few games in there, but his motivation would not change. He would still want to score goals, and his character would be no different, but his ability to do his job would be greatly reduced.

You can't expect to win every race you enter, or every championship that you challenge for, and putting up with the setbacks is part of a driver's skill as well. The disappointments will always outweigh the triumphs – even Jim Clark lost more races than he won. If you win all the time, you are probably doing something that is too easy, something that is not pushing you sufficiently.

Whatever the machinery, though, you clearly have to try your best, whether that is in a struggling Grand Prix car, as a Formula Ford backmarker or as the best bike rider on the grid. The point of any kind of racing is to push yourself as hard as possible, and that is what I did from the moment I got into my first racing car. The motivation for any racing driver worth his salt is the same – we all want to get the best from ourselves and our cars, and we all want to win.

That's the beauty of Formula One – it's the top level, the ultimate challenge. In America, the IndyCar series might have one or two exceptionally good drivers, but there will always be at least four or five of that calibre racing in Formula One, and a lot more who are banging on the door of being exceptional. To beat those people gives you the sort of buzz that you do not get from anything else, a feeling of pure satisfaction at having done the very best you could, of fulfilment, of completion. Despite the risks and the sacrifices, those are the moments that keep us all coming back for more.

It doesn't always work out as you would like. You can always try your best, but if the machinery is so bad that you are going backwards in races, then your ability to compete is

Beauty and
the beast,
Monaco 1992
with Brabham

In the fast-changing, whirlwind world of Formula One, the right image can be the making of both teams and drivers. Being stigmatised is not a good career move. Each team tries to give the impression of being the best-oiled machine and each driver likes to appear the coolest and the most in control, but behind the façade everyone is working their buns off to succeed.

We know that motor racing is a glamorous sport, because that's what we're told all the time, but sometimes it is hard to see the glamour for the grit. Every now and then, you find yourself at some far-flung racetrack, putting on a cold, sweat-drenched balaclava for the tenth time, exhausted after driving for the fourth day in a row and wanting nothing more out of life than some dry clothes and a mug of tea. Glamour? Not this time.

None of us would be involved in Formula One if we did not enjoy the sport, but it can be easy to forget the image we project. As drivers, our focus is on winning races, and the way to do that is to concentrate our attention on aerodynamic tweaks, tyre compounds, test sessions, engines and such like. That leaves precious little time for the showbiz lifestyle people imagine we lead, because I don't think there is any driver who'd rather be drinking a cocktail when he could be making his car go faster.

Still, the old-fashioned image of the racing driver persists, fed by all those familiar images from years gone by. Think of Formula One, and most people conjure up the image of a speeding Ferrari dashing around the Monaco Grand Prix circuit with a playboy at the wheel – the same playboy who turned up in his yacht just before the race, jumped in the car without a care in the world and then reeled off seventy daredevil laps before dinner. We like to believe that myth, but the truth is that those types were not usually the most successful.

Historically, Formula One was the playground of the rich and famous, because you needed to be wealthy or remarkably talented to succeed. There was an almost aristocratic feel to the sport, with barons, counts, dukes and various heirs lining up on the grid along with a few monied types and a handful of gentleman racers, and that image has stuck. These days, though, that image is played up because so many people want to present our sport as one that is fuelled by glamour and exclusivity as much as it is by sponsorship and horsepower. The teams make themselves attractive to sponsors and then the sponsors want to get the biggest return from their investment. And, perhaps, there are a couple of drivers who like the world to think of them as daring playboys. Indeed, I wouldn't mind being one myself!

IMAGE

Image is ultimately what sells Formula One, and the Monaco Grand Prix is the prime example. It might be a faintly absurd place in which to stage a race, but Monaco is crucial to the health of Formula One. Think of this single race, and you'll find yourself thinking about wealth, glitz and glamour, and a circuit that winds its way past some of the best-known motor racing landmarks anywhere in the world. The Monaco Grand Prix is known everywhere on the planet.

It can be lovely, and if you're running well in Monaco the world can seem a perfect place. Unfortunately, last season that was not the case. In fact, it was a thoroughly miserable experience because the whole weekend was a disaster for everybody at Jordan. Ralf Schumacher and I qualified towards the back of the grid, ran around at the rear of the field for the whole race, and just about managed to avoid finishing last, with me cursing the car for its ill-timed reliability – I was hoping that it would break down in familiar style, but it just kept going for lap after lacklustre lap. The whole event was nothing more than damn hard work for pretty little gain.

> *"Image is ultimately what sells Formula One, and the Monaco Grand Prix is the prime example."*

Monaco's small size makes it a tough place to go racing under any circumstances, and when things are against you it can be very depressing and claustrophobic. The pit garages are tiny, the paddock is cramped and it can take an age to get from one place to another. It's a legacy of another era, when teams had less equipment to take to every race and the whole thing was a bit more *ad hoc*. In the modern era, Monaco's facilities are just not suitable, but you have to do the best you can, even if it does drive you mad. We have enough work to do on the car without having to do it in a garage the size of a lift.

And I get paid for this?

Lear 31a – you really ought
to get one of these

F1's crown jewel . . . Monaco

The pit-lane is far too tight and it's crawling with guests, journalists and sponsors – Monaco is the one race of the year that everybody seems to want to attend. It's hard to move around without somebody wanting to talk to you. Although the attention is something we're used to, it tends to get a bit out of control in Monte Carlo. If you're not careful, you can spend too much time shaking hands, and not enough preparing your car.

Not that racing is the only thing that people have on their minds. The Grand Prix usually coincides with the Cannes Film Festival and the grid is always crammed with starlets and film stars, standing around and being seen in the right places. Anybody who thinks they are anybody turns up in Monaco for the Grand Prix weekend and a lot of them are far more interested in the business of 'see and be seen' than they are in the cars. It can be quite a feat to drive your car down the packed pit-lane without mowing down half the royal families of Europe! Thank goodness they've imposed a speed limit, or we could easily have had a rather gory diplomatic incident by now.

All these famous visitors are very good for the magazine photographers, who can get a clutch of them at the same time, but I sometimes wonder how many of these people actually understand what it is all about. This year, one celebrity was standing around before the start of the race and somebody asked him who he thought would win. 'If it rains,' he said, 'I reckon David Schumacher will do it.'

One particular celebrity even made a habit of coming to races all season long. Throughout the year, we would see Sylvester Stallone wandering around, soaking up the

**With Peter Boutwood
my design guru**

atmosphere, taking notes and chatting to as many people as he could. He was making preparations for a film about Formula One, which, no doubt, will give the sport an even greater prominence in the US market that Formula One covets (particularly given that he is one of the biggest film

**When Bernie listens,
people talk**

arranging the television rights and generally creating the whole enterprise that billions of people around the world tune in to see on television.

Bernie has made a prodigious fortune out of motor racing and he became the highest-paid company director in British history when his salary peaked at £1m per week – not bad for a man who was once a second-hand motorbike salesman on the Old Kent Road. He has an instinctive understanding of the way the sport works, and it was his appreciation of how all the elements fit together that enabled the sport to grow to such an enormous and profitable level. We are the modern-day Ben Hurs taking part in a chariot race that is beamed around the world, but we are just part of the show and we know it. At the top of it all sits Bernie, looking down on the Circus Maximus that he created, and Monaco is the jewel in his crown.

stars in the world and would be producing the movie and acting in it). Among all the people in Formula One, Bernie Ecclestone is the main one making sure that the sport keeps on growing and, with an eye on that American market (which Formula One really needs to crack if it is ever going to live up to that world championship tag), it's probably safe to say that he helped Stallone out as much as possible. After all, he's smart enough to see that a glossy, big-budget feature film is just what the sport, and the ever-important sponsors, wants.

Bernie is the mastermind behind the packaging and selling of the whole Formula One brand. He's the pivotal figure in the success of the sport, just as he has been for the best part of two decades, striking deals with all the teams,

The race will always find a place on any Formula One calendar because of its fame and its historical standing. With all those sponsors coming in droves, you can be sure of being invited to a series of functions in the evenings and, since these are the people who keep the money rolling into motor racing's coffers, it would be churlish not to attend. It's part of my job to represent my team and entertain guests as best I can, but the problem is that I normally have only half a mind on the job at hand. At Monte Carlo, you can't stop thinking about the problems you are going to come up against in the coming days.

Monaco is like that, not just for me, but for all the drivers I know. It provides a unique challenge and it preys on your mind. Some people love driving there because it's so unusual and some hate it for the same reasons, but everybody spends the weekend thinking about the challenges that lie ahead, rolling them over in their minds.

"For sheer evocative power, there is only one name in Formula One that challenges Monaco's position and that, of course, is Ferrari."

Driving there requires a greater degree of concentration than any other race on the calendar. There are myriad difficulties that can take you by surprise – barriers that you could clip and end your race, corners that force you to slow down to what feels like walking pace, and a surface so bumpy that you feel as if you are about to be thrown out of the car. It's impossible to test at Monaco, of course, and there is no similar circuit to allow you to prepare, so every year we have to re-familiarise ourselves with its idiosyncrasies. If you can get through the weekend without encountering some kind of trouble, you're entitled to feel very happy.

For sheer evocative power, there is only one name in Formula One that challenges Monaco's position and that, of course, is Ferrari. Put them together, and you have something remarkable – Grand Prix racing's most glamorous team competing at its most glamorous location. However

A street car named Desire

Getting out
of a tight spot –
a Monaco pit lane

commercial the sport may become, the sight of the red car charging through Casino Square is as evocative now as it ever has been.

The image of Formula One is built upon the legend of Ferrari and, for the moment, the reputation of Michael Schumacher. They embody many of the key ingredients that are then sold around the world. On top of that, you have teams like Benetton and Jordan, who have an appeal of their own.

As much as Michael Schumacher, or any other driver for that matter, means to Formula One, Ferrari is the heart of the sport, known all over the world. Whatever happens, people will always talk about Ferrari with a sense of awe. If the team wins a Grand Prix, the reports make the sports headlines in just about every country in the world – including, of course, the United States.

I would be lying if I said that I was more immune to the Ferrari legend than anybody else, and if the chance had come up I would love to have driven for the team. The feeling of having driven a Ferrari in a Grand Prix would be something you would carry for ever, something you could bore your grandchildren with for hours on end. Your photograph would be there in the record books and you would take your place in the team's coveted history. However hard-nosed we might like to imagine ourselves, there are not many people who would be able to turn their back on an offer to drive for Formula One's most famous team.

The trouble is that if you do take their offer, it comes with a caveat. Plenty of good drivers have discovered over the

**Nowhere else gives
the same impression
of speed**

years that if you're not competitive behind the wheel of a Ferrari, your life can be hell. The attention is remorseless. One of the Italian newspapers carries at least one page of Ferrari news every day of the year, and many, many more after each race, so the drivers are always under a microscope, being probed for weaknesses. The fortunes of the Ferrari team have a quasi-religious importance for many people in Italy, so if you're winning races, then you're a hero, but when things are not going well, then the attention, and the criticism, can be unending. If the driver in question happens to be Italian, the pressure is far worse.

The value of the team will never change though, for Ferrari's strength lies in its history. The first time a child sees a picture of a racing car, it will almost certainly be red, and from that nebulous beginning comes the love for Ferrari. I am not sure whether Ferrari were lucky that they tapped into a subconscious connection between speed and the colour red, or whether the world has decided that a Ferrari is the perfect image of a fast car, but the result is

Tifosi

the same. Think of a fast car, and you invariably think of a Ferrari, so when you apply that emotion to sport, you're bound to come up with images of speed, glamour, money and the golden era of motor racing.

Companies such as Mercedes and Ford also help to maintain that tradition, stirring up memories of how the sport was in decades past and reminding us of the feats of our predecessors, but it is the Ferrari name that matters most. Whatever the truth may be about the business of motor racing, the important thing is to make it seem chic and glamorous, and that is why Ferrari, with all the associations that go with that name, is so vital to Formula One. Without that single team, the image of Grand Prix motor racing would suffer terribly, which is why so many people are keen to see Ferrari succeed.

Strip away the mythology, though, and the present Ferrari team is an interesting hybrid, headed up by the same people who were at Benetton until 1996. In years gone by,

**My father on his way to a
record fifth Monaco victory**

**Father of
the legend,
Enzo Ferrari**

it was Enzo Ferrari who ruled the roost, but the present team is largely run by Jean Todt, who is French, and the Englishman Ross Brawn. They have an Australian designer, Rory Byrne, German and Irish drivers and the car is largely paid for by Marlboro and Shell, companies based in America and Holland. Indeed, there's not much Italian about the roots of their car, except for the location of the factory. That, though, doesn't seem to matter much, and the track invasion after the team's 1–2 in Monza was one of the most emotional sights motor racing has produced in years. The name and the image of Ferrari are as strong, and as Italian, as ever.

In fact, manufacturers are becoming more important than ever in Formula One, and as that happens, the role of the driver is changing. In the mid-1960s, it was the driver who was the most important star of the show, but now we are becoming more like jockeys in horse racing who are hired to use their skills but are still not seen as the most important element in a winning package. We're well paid, of course, and the public still look to the drivers first, but there are a lot of people within Formula One who place the driver below chassis, engine and tyres on their wishlists. Get the horse right, and then find a jockey to ride it. We're like jockeys in another way too, because we have to travel far and wide to do our job. One year I spent a total of twelve complete days in mid-air. That's nearly 300 hours on a plane, and that number is getting higher with each passing season as we test abroad with an ever greater frequency.

'Pizza Hut . . . Can you deliver
to 30,000 feet?'

The truth is that, for most of the European races, I arrive and go straight from the airport to the circuit, then to the hotel, then back to the circuit, and I keep up that routine until the race is over and I go home. That goes for testing as well, so although I have been to many different countries, there is not much that I could tell you about them.

I have a wife, four children and a lovely house in Ireland that I like to spend time in, but my job means I am away for much of the year. Instead, I end up expending a lot of energy thinking of ways to get home as soon as possible. Only when I am back with my family do I really relax, which is important to me both as a driver and a person. The job of a racing driver is a pretty stressful one, and you need to turn off from those pressures and forget them. Relaxing, believe it or not, is actually very important in keeping me motivated and fresh for the challenge.

There is a rule that says you cannot test in the week before a Grand Prix. The knock-on effect is that now, after a three-day Grand Prix meeting, I normally come home for a day before flying off again to another test, in another country. After that, I get to go home for the weekend and then start to prepare for the next race, all assuming that I don't have to go somewhere else for a sponsor's engagement. It is, by anyone's standards, hectic.

There's training to be done as well, and other business work that needs to be taken care of, and it is easy to end up exhausted. That's when it's difficult to see the glamorous side to Formula One and that's why so many drivers concentrate on doing whatever they can to make their lives a little less hectic.

Take private jets – I do! Of course they're a luxury, but they have become almost a necessity for a lot of the drivers in Formula One. If you add up all the time you would otherwise spend waiting at airports, checking in and then waiting through the inevitable delays, it can all add considerably to the workload and stress of the job, taking its toll on you before you even arrive at the track. With your own plane, you can leave when you want, land where you want and arrive feeling pretty good, which shows itself on the track. Like so much else in this sport, it has a glamorous exterior, but a very pragmatic core.

The fact is that, more and more, you have to be completely focused on looking after your own well-being. You need to be organised, thoughtful and fit, and none of that comes very easily.

Fitness training is vital, and it puts another restriction on our efforts to chase this promised glamorous lifestyle. I am not sure you would last long in Formula One if you went out nightclubbing and living to excess in the midst of a Grand Prix season. The man who goes out on a mighty bender before the Hungarian Grand Prix, for instance, would be the man full of regret when he got to the halfway mark of one of the toughest races of the year, sweating out his hangover in 40°C heat.

If you wilt, there's nobody to hold your hand, because motor racing is a very solitary sport once the race has started. It's not like being a footballer, where you have another ten guys to help you out if things aren't going well. A Grand Prix is normally the best part of two hours long, with no half-time break, and that makes it more like running a marathon than anything else – and marathon runners don't have to wear flameproof overalls.

Formula One is like any other athletic event, except that we do our sport sitting down. It's demanding, hard work, where the onus is on isometric tension – which means that, instead of using your muscles to move something, you are actually using your strength to hold yourself in position. A driver has to be fit enough to stay tense when there is a big load going through his body, and that uses up a lot of energy. In Imola, for instance, I lost two litres of fluid just through sweating – that's nearly four pints of water coming out of my body over the course of an hour and a half. It's a brave person who gives a driver a hug after a race. In August, I had a test at Jerez in Spain where it was 40°C and hardly ideal conditions. In order to keep myself from dehydrating, I had to drink seven litres of fluid a day or else I would have dried up completely. Being clad in three layers of fireproof racing overalls on a blazing hot day is as far as you can get from lying by the pool with your swimming trunks on and a cold beer in your hand.

How fit are we, though? I am often asked to compare a racing driver's fitness with that of other sportsmen, and it's tough to say because each sport places different demands on its participants. A long-distance runner might be useless in a game of football, for instance, because he would not be able to sprint fast enough over short distances. Swimmers train hard, but may not be able to run a marathon very well, while a weightlifter who can lift vast amounts would probably look pretty sluggish over a 400-metre race. What counts is concentrating on the demands of your own discipline. Mind you, I doubt that there are many other sportsmen in the world who could do more than a couple of laps in a racing car without their necks giving up and their heart rate going through the roof.

Driving a Formula One car is a constant battle. You accelerate, brake and corner so quickly that you are constantly fighting the extreme G-forces exerted on your body, pushing you from one side to another, trying to throw you out of your seat. While you are coping with that, you have to deal with the bumps that crop up on every circuit, especially Monaco, bumps that shake you so badly that, after an hour, you can start to feel mildly concussed. It is like riding a bicycle down a set of stairs for an hour and a half, or roller-skating over a cobbled street.

Nevertheless, Formula One is all about thrills and Monaco is about as thrilling as it can get. Some of the most evocative images in the sport are of Grand Prix cars flowing through the tight turns and over the crests and curves of the beautiful principality. Formula One is part sport, part business and part entertainment, with Monaco and Ferrari up there in lights at the top of the bill and the rest of us fighting for a slice of the action. It might not be quite so glamorous when we're looking at it from behind the scenes, but when we sit down and think about all the history and emotion, the characters and the thrills, we can't help but be secretly proud to be part of one of the greatest shows on earth.

**After qualifying for the
Austrian Grand Prix**

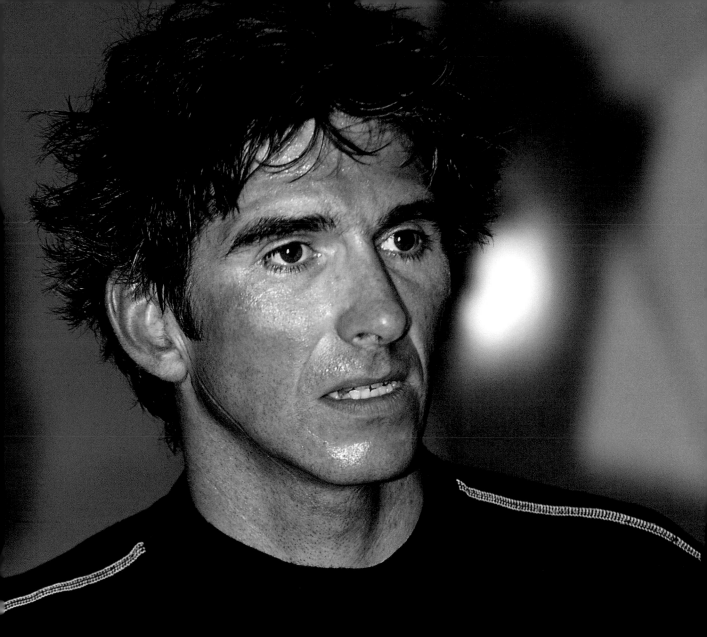

enjoy racing in Canada. The people there have a tremendously positive attitude, full of hope, which, after the season we had had, was just what I needed.

I was in the lift at my hotel a couple of days before the race and a guy walked in and stared at me, and then began to smile. 'How are you going to do then, Damon?' he asked me. I was a bit ambivalent, mumbling something about not holding out that much hope. The guy didn't stop smiling for a moment, but he looked surprised. 'You're in the race, aren't you?' he said. 'Yes,' I replied, and the guy smiled even more. 'Well then, you've got a chance,' he said, and got out at the next floor. By the time I reached my room, I was feeling more bullish than ever, and as it turned out, I nearly got on the podium. Golden rule: anything can happen in Formula One – just don't give up hope. The race in Montreal was restarted after an enormous accident and that set the pattern for the afternoon. It seemed like a driver was going off just about every lap and, by the simple expedient of keeping clear of trouble, I managed to get up to third place before my first pit-stop. Everything was looking good for a top-three finish, which would have done everybody at Jordan, including myself, the power of good. Then our bad luck struck again and the car dribbled to a halt.

If that was disappointing, then what happened after the race had finished was depressingly familiar. I had had a little battle with Michael Schumacher when we were contesting second place and, before I knew it, he had said in a press conference that I had tried to kill him by weaving all over the road when he was trying to pass me. He really did say that. He suggested, with a straight face, that my driving could have killed him. No matter that, in the same race, Michael had knocked Heinz-Harald Frentzen off the track, or that he himself had weaved in front of me lots of times in the past. No, he said that I had done my best to kill him and everybody listened agog. Not surprisingly, the world's Press absolutely feasted on the story. Hill and Schumacher were, it seemed, back at each other's throats, which was just the sort of story that everybody loves.

In fact, it wasn't the first time we had clashed in the season. At the first race, in Melbourne, I came out of the pits while Michael was on a quick lap and I got in his way at the first corner. I tried my hardest to leave him a way through, but it wasn't enough. There was nothing I could do about it, but, on television, it looked for all the world as if I was deliberately holding him up. It looked like it to Schumacher, too, because he drove alongside me, shaking his fist.

How many times have we seen that before from Michael? Personally, I have seen it more than enough, so I thought to myself 'I'm not taking this' and drove off. Lo and behold, the next thing I know, he's racing me into the next corner, obviously wound up. And at that precise moment, the television cameras picked us up and started broadcasting our little tiff to the whole world.

**The moment before
my 'assassination' attempt
on Michael Schumacher**

Formula One is about sport and it's about entertainment. It's about giving people what they want, satisfying all their curiosities and keeping them gripped. There are a lot of sides to that, but, as with any other sport, one of the aspects that spectators like to see is a good bit of rivalry. They want to see drivers battling against each other with a bit of bite. And, this being Formula One, they normally get it.

Rivalries develop as time goes by. Drivers tend, at some point, to give their opinion on other drivers and they also tend not to be too complimentary while they're at it. That's part of the fabric of the sport.

It is just about impossible for any driver to compliment another one without being made to feel that he has stepped out of line. It's just not the done thing, because we're all worried about seeming weak. The natural reaction is to play down the skill of the others and hope that, in turn, your own reputation goes up.

That might sound like quite acceptable business practice but, as time passes, all those comments begin to grate. It gets on your nerves to constantly hear yourself being bad-mouthed and criticised, and eventually something inside snaps. If somebody keeps having a go at you, then your reaction is to say: 'I'll show him.'

There is a difference, though, between spats – where it's just a couple of drivers who have had a few words about something – and genuine, hard-fought rivalries that have a real edge. For them, you need some extra factor that has thrown a couple of guys together, something that

makes them want to beat each other more than anybody else in the field. What that normally means is that they are either team-mates or they are the two challengers for the world championship, because those are the key conflicts that make up Formula One.

There have been two of them in my Formula One career, two rivalries that have been played out in front of a worldwide audience. Both of them have been keenly fought, and both of them taught me a lot about the way the sport operates. The other drivers involved in them? Jacques Villeneuve and, of course, Michael Schumacher.

I have lost count of the number of times I have tussled with Michael over the past four seasons, and there is no doubt that our rivalry has come under a lot of scrutiny at various times. But I also had a great year when I was battling at the front with Jacques Villeneuve, a season that

ended with me edging him out to become world champion. From the outside, the battles might have looked similar, but from my point of view there was a world of difference.

With Jacques, most obviously, we were fighting as team-mates and also fighting for the championship. It's hard enough to deal with a fast team-mate, but when that guy is also your rival for the title, then there's a lot at stake. You have to do your best to stay on top of everything, to stay in control.

Sometimes, competitive team-mates can mean double-trouble for a team. Giancarlo Fisichella, for example, clearly did not hit it off with Ralf Schumacher at all well at Jordan last year and that probably did not help them. Both of them were desperate to win their own personal duel and, instead of concentrating all their attention on the races, they both spent rather too long thinking of ways to beat

Team-mates?
Ralf Schumacher
and Giancarlo
Fisichella

RIVALRY

each other. For everybody involved, that's a difficult situation to deal with.

Sometimes, though, it can be very healthy, and that was the case during my battles with Jacques while we were together at Williams in 1996. Even though we were both fighting for the biggest prizes, we didn't end up hating each other or trying to knock each other off the track. It was a good battle, a good rivalry and it provided people with good entertainment.

I like Jacques and I respect him. He has a very strong sense of sportsmanship and he is always keen to maintain that element of fairness that some of the other drivers don't

Hard but fair,
Jacques Villeneuve

"An ideal relationship is one where you have a certain regard for your competitors and earn their respect by your own performance."

worry about. If you beat Jacques in a race or outdo him somehow, he doesn't take it personally. He's big enough to shake your hand and say well done. To him, that's part of life and part of the sport, and it means that if he beats you in the next race, you return the compliment.

Now, despite all this friendship, there was still plenty of competition between us. Sure we got on well as team-mates, but the rivalry was still intense within the team and we were both desperate to win. I wanted to win the world championship and so did he, and there was no way that either of us was going to lose sight of that.

He would never offer to help me, and I would never offer to help him, and we both knew that those were the rules. To him, it was a case of all being fair in love and war, and he wouldn't hesitate to try to distract me somehow. If something annoyed me or put me off, I always expected Jacques to take advantage of that and exploit it, but I never felt bitter. On the track, I always knew he would be fair, but I would never expect him to wave me past. That's what makes for a good rivalry and, after I had beaten him to the championship, Jacques offered me a warm handshake to say well done. The following season, I was pleased to see him succeed me as world champion.

122

I have a similar relationship with Ralf Schmacher now and I'm delighted that it has developed that way. We are both aware that neither of us is going to make it easy for the other guy, but at the same time we are not going to be stupid about it and deliberately try to withhold information or be pig-headed. There is a line that, as team-mates, you shouldn't cross.

The important thing in a rivalry is that you try to understand the other person and get a handle on how they behave. Motor racing is a lot safer these days, but it remains a dangerous sport, and I feel a lot happier if I'm racing hard against someone whom I respect.

The acid test is whether the person you're up against is the sort of guy who is going to be able to get out of his car at the end of the race and say 'I enjoyed that.' He might go on to say 'You shouldn't have done that' or 'I'm sorry, but I shouldn't have done that', but if you can sit down and have a chat and a laugh afterwards, then that's as much as you can realistically ask for. An ideal relationship is one where you have a certain regard for your

"There is a line that, as team-mates, you shouldn't cross."

competitors and earn their respect by your own performance. Jacques is a great example of somebody who acts
properly when he is racing with you. I'm not so sure about
a few others.

A couple of years ago, Jacques overtook Michael Schumacher while they were going round the outside of a bend
in Estoril. It was a brilliant piece of driving and it got people
up out of their seats and cheering all over the world. When
I saw a replay of it on television a little later on, I was pretty
impressed myself, because it was a brave, instinctive
manoeuvre – just what motor racing at the very top level
is all about.

The two of them were running very close and Michael got
himself tangled up, briefly, with a backmarker. Immediately, Jacques seized the opportunity and took the corner,
but Michael just couldn't bring himself to say well done
after the race had finished.

What Michael should have said was 'that was close but
well done, you caught me napping.' Instead, he complained
to him about it and claimed Jacques' manoeuvre was
dangerous. While everybody else was patting Jacques on
the back, Michael was trying to rubbish him. If he had
considered Jacques' move to be dangerous, then he should
have backed off instead of waiting to moan about it.
Michael felt he had to criticise Jacques for what he did
simply because, on the day, he had been beaten fair and
square – and that is not the right approach at all.

**A crack
in the ice**

In the blue corner . . .

There are two things that set Michael apart from the rest of the drivers in Formula One – his sheer talent and his attitude. I am full of admiration for the former, but the latter leaves me cold.

> "There are two things that set Michael apart from the rest of the drivers in Formula One – his sheer talent and his attitude."

When it comes to his driving, though, I don't mind being complimentary. He is perceived to be the most extraordinarily talented driver in Formula One and it would be daft to pretend that he is not very good. That does not mean he cannot be beaten or challenged, though, because it would mean more to beat him than anybody else because he is perceived to be the best.

Eddie Irvine, who has been his team-mate at Ferrari for the past three years, is not somebody I normally agree with, but he has got one thing right. Irvine takes the view that Michael is incredible and he accepts that and tries to get on with the job of approaching him for speed.

Other team-mates, up until then, have been totally outpsyched by their inability to cope with being second to Michael and being soundly beaten. They might have been given lesser equipment or shown less interest by the team, but they have made matters worse by not coming to terms with that. From the start, Irvine grasped the nettle and said okay, I have to make it my objective to be as close as I can. That is the only way a driver can cope with being put up against Schumacher.

1994 was the year when the rivalry between Michael and me came to a head, and that was the year when I first became really aware of what a talent he has.

I had a conversation with Michael in the paddock and I told him that I thought he had a lot of talent. It was just after Benetton had had all their stuff impounded amid allegations that they were using traction control. I said to him that he was good enough not to need any kind of illegal help and it would not help him in the long run. He is there to win however he can do it. Some of his victories are brilliant. Some of his methods, though, are very questionable.

The difference between the rivalry between Ayrton Senna and Alain Proust and mine with Michael is that I was never held in esteem by Michael. His attitude is a bit like Goliath. He is full of disdain for his enemies and the challenge they present, as if he is saying, 'Why do you bring me these mere mortals?' It doesn't rest easily with him to pay compliments to his rivals.

Throughout the 1994 season, there had been suggestions and rumours that Michael had not been playing it straight, so it was acrimonious from the start. Then you add to that his problems with ignoring the black flag in Silverstone and you could see how it was taking shape.

A great 'sporting' moment?

The whole season was acted out under a cloud from Imola, where Ayrton Senna and Roland Ratzenberger had both died in crashes. After that came Michael's attempts to undermine me through the papers by saying I was not a very good driver. It all added to the rivalry and, of course, a lot of people loved it.

Formula One can be a little like boxing. It usually comes down to a conflict between two drivers for the championship and, as in boxing, it is more interesting to see a fight between two guys who hate each other's guts than two blokes who think the world of each other. I remember seeing Nigel Benn and Chris Eubank on a chat show before a fight and they were being set up to show they had respect for each other, but it didn't ring true and consequently it diffused the whole event. You need someone like Mohammad Ali to say 'I'm the greatest and the other guy is ugly and slow.' He, however, managed to do it in a way that endeared him to people.

In 1994, we had a climax whereby the championship would be over if I didn't beat Michael in the penultimate race. I beat him fair and square in Japan in the rain and I believe to this day that we had equal machinery then. I even did one pit-stop where they could not get one of the rear tyres off, so I had one tyre that did the whole race. It was exciting and it set up the final race in Adelaide as the decider. I went away on a high and Michael had to delay his celebrations.

We all know what happened next in Adelaide. He was forced to push so hard that he made a mistake which could have cost him the world championship if it was not for

**No compromise,
Silverstone 1995**

the fact that his car had enough left in it so that he could drive into me as I went to pass him. I didn't have to say anything. Everyone saw what had happened and I just knew there was no point in saying anything at that time. I was not going to let the season end with people calling me a sore loser. It had been a pretty tragic season anyway and everyone was already outraged at what he had done. I just thought I would leave it at that.

At the time, I couldn't believe that he would do such a thing but, with hindsight, I think I was being a little naïve. I was not going to accuse him of doing the dirty on me, because I regarded it as an error of judgment on my part. I simply had not understood how far some drivers – and one driver in particular – would go in order to win. I was shocked that

RIVALRY

Bitter rivals, Alain Prost and Ayrton Senna

What it did do was to make Michael champion, but at the same time it painted him pretty much as the villain in many people's eyes, particularly in the UK. He was the champion, no doubt about that, but he had not achieved it in the way that a champion should.

The rivalry was kept alive, not out of any deliberate intention on my part, but because we happened to be the protagonists again the following year. The whole season was a repeat performance of Adelaide and the Press were always trying to get me to say what I thought about him.

My line was 'Don't get mad, get even'. The scene was set in 1995 for it to be a return match. As it turned out, it was one of the worst seasons I have ever had.

anybody would resort to that, but there was nothing I could accomplish. I simply filed it away for future reference.

I was new to the game. It was only my second season in Formula One and I was not sure how to deal with all the questions. My friends around me told me not to say a thing and that was the best advice I was given. It was not necessary for me to say anything and it would not have changed what happened.

A juvenile part of me wanted to have a rivalry and I was quite happy for it to be Damon v Michael, because everyone was singing his praises and telling me what a great driver he was. I wanted to beat Michael and earn some respect for myself. But I misjudged the situation and, in a way, it put me in the same predicament as some of his team-mates, in that I was his preferred victim. If you lose to him, you tend to find yourself in the firing line while the other guys do not even get a mention. There is a price to

pay for pitching yourself against the best. You have to win and the pressure is greater. In 1995, I didn't win. In fact, I came off very badly.

I was not experienced enough and I didn't appreciate what Frank Williams and Patrick Head wanted and how they worked. My mistake was to assume that they would back me up in my personal battle in the drivers' championship against Schumacher. Where it seems I got things wrong was in assuming that they were interested in the drivers' championship at all. To them, Formula One is about providing the best equipment to the drivers and then letting them get on with it. The constructors' championship, with its fringe benefits, such as where a team can park in the paddock and garage their cars, the bonuses paid by sponsors and manufacturers, moving up the pecking order for new deals and, of course, the satisfaction of outperforming a rival, is everything to a team owner.

In effect, I was left to my own devices to beat the Schumacher–Benetton war machine. Benetton's focus was on the drivers' championship and giving Michael every advantage wherever possible, even if that meant the other driver in the team lost out, and they ended up winning both the drivers' and constructors' titles. That was when the seeds of my departure from Williams the following season were sown, because I ended the year as a beaten man. As a campaign, 1995 nearly ended my career as a Grand Prix driver, all because I lost to my main rival.

In Formula One, the driving is the easy bit – politics and all the other outside stresses are what really test a modern driver. It is about how you can stay unaffected by all the

other aspects of the sport and it is not so easy to push all those concerns to one side. It is the difference between walking along a tightrope when it's a foot off the ground, and doing it when it's slung between two buildings 500 feet up in the air. That's when the people who can are sorted from those who just think they can.

> "There is a price to pay for pitching yourself against the best. You have to win and the pressure is greater."

For some people, the political side to the sport comes as second nature and that gives them a big advantage over the rest. They can deal with all the battles that are going on behind the scenes and manipulate them to their own advantage. While the rest of the field are fretting and worrying, there are normally a couple of canny drivers who have everything worked out. Put somebody like that into a bitter rivalry, and it's something to behold!

Alain Prost was a master at dealing with all those outside influences and pressures, so when he was paired with Ayrton Senna at McLaren their battle was destined to be a classic.

With both those men behind the wheel of a good car (with what was easily the best engine), McLaren won all but one of the races in 1988 and only some very bad luck

"In Formula One, the driving is the easy bit - politics and all the other outside stresses are what really test a modern driver."

prevented them winning the other race as well. It was complete domination, an absolute two-horse race, and a lot of people took the view that it was not very interesting. I thought it was fascinating to watch because you didn't know which man would win each race, but you could see they both wanted desperately to come out on top.

The fact that the two best drivers of the time were in the same team created a tinderbox situation because they had this ferocious rivalry, which was nearly all aggravated by Ayrton.

He had a vulnerability about him, as I discovered when we worked together in 1994. He readily flew off the handle if he suspected he was being mistreated and, at times in 1988, he obviously felt that Alain, somehow or other, was pulling a fast one on him. Ayrton would come out with these emotional outbursts, demanding justice but, more than that, showing his weak points to everybody around. The more angry Ayrton got, the more obvious it was to Alain, and everybody else, that he was worried.

The story of their rivalry became even more interesting to me because I worked with both drivers in the following

years. Alain was my Williams team-mate in 1993 and Ayrton replaced him the next year and I discovered for myself that they were entirely different characters. Alain was a more considered, thoughtful person, someone who made his point through innuendo rather than thumping the table. Ayrton, on the other hand, was impulsive and much more likely to do something without thinking of the consequences.

In that amazing 1988 season you got the impression that Alain was a little bit smarter at playing with politics and more in control. Ayrton, by contrast, always seemed to be at his limit all the time, always wound up and ready to let go. That was how Ayrton was anyway, but Prost managed to push him into corners and get him excited and frustrated, playing on his flaws.

Ayrton's volatile nature has revealed itself a few times over the years. A couple of seasons later, for instance, Ayrton hit Eddie Irvine in the face after a race because he was angry with him. If he had been in control, Ayrton would not have given him the time of day, but he was goaded into doing it by a mischievous Gerhard Berger, his team-mate at the time. Ayrton couldn't help it, because that was

**Senna's *raison
d'être* – to beat Prost**

**The last resort, Jacques Villeneuve
and Michael Schumacher, Jerez 1997**

"I have never felt that hatred for the other guy is a healthy emotion."

the way he was, but it gave Prost a chink in the Senna armour that he could exploit. And, of course, he exploited it to the full.

Their rivalry was an absolute classic. It featured two great characters and it had a purpose. It wasn't just that they were team-mates, not even that they were both fighting for the world championship. Instead, it was all about the two of them trying to outdo each other and prove to the world which of them was the best racing driver in Formula One.

Ayrton was the pretender because, at that time, Alain was the one who had the bigger reputation. He was regarded as the best driver around and, as Ayrton well knew, if you want to become the best, you have to beat the best. You have to demolish other people's icon, the person who has become popular and a model of perfection. If you can't do that, then the question of who is top-dog comes down to conjecture and personal preference. If you thrash your nearest rival, nobody doubts that you are the best.

So how do you create a good rivalry? Certainly not by hatred. I have never felt that hatred for the other guy is a healthy emotion. I think intense desire to beat someone, perhaps stemming from dislike, is fine, but you shouldn't be motivated by out and out hatred.

You have to harness your emotions if you are to be effective. You cannot let them rule you or else you are out of control and in no fit state to be racing. Mario Andretti got it right when he said that you have to be angry, but you should not get angry in a racing car. You need controlled aggression. If you get angry, you're in the wall.

It doesn't matter what sport it is, you normally get a better performance out of two guys who have an intense rivalry. Sebastian Coe and Steve Ovett, for instance. It was always a showdown. Two men give their absolute best when they know they can't afford to lose.

If you are regularly beaten in Formula One, you are basically finished as a racing driver. It doesn't take long for a reputation to slip away and the important thing is to make sure that it's not yours that's slipping. That's why rivalry is a key part of the sport, and that's why it's so vital for any driver that he comes out on top. Whether it's against his team-mate or a championship rival, friendship dissolves into nothing from Friday to Sunday. As Gore Vidal said, rather bitterly, 'whenever a friend succeeds, a little something in me dies.' In Formula One, that may well be true.

I wouldn't like to guess how many days I have spent driving around Silverstone in my life, but it must be hundreds. Nevertheless, there is something very special about going there in the middle of July for the British Grand Prix, the one chance we have to drive in front of a home crowd. However seasoned you are, it is still a moving experience to see the banners and flags all around the circuit, and it's a potent reminder that, whatever happens on the track, there are a lot of really devoted Formula One fans.

At every British Grand Prix, I feel a tremendous sense of expectancy from the crowd which, in turn, gives me the feeling that I have a duty to give them my best. This year, I came to Silverstone without a point, yet the support was undiminished.

Support like that adds a certain amount of pressure, but how could you not enjoy the feeling of people wishing you well? The problem comes when it's time to repay the favour by signing autographs and posing for photographs. Although I don't mind doing it, I simply do not have time to sign everyone's autograph book. There simply are not enough hours in the day.

I am at the race, more than anything, to try to do well on the track. I have to spend time with the team, setting up the car and talking to the engineers. As the cars become more and more complicated, so those briefings go on ever longer. When I'm dashing through the Silverstone gates, it's not because I want to get away from the fans – I'm probably just late for a meeting.

In the end, I often feel bad about signing even the few autographs that I can manage, because it means disappointing the many people who didn't get their chance. I know that fans queue up from early in the morning and, as I sign some autographs on the way in, I can't help feeling that I'm bound to miss out the person who has waited the longest. In the end, it becomes an impossible task to give everyone what they want. All you can do is say 'sorry'.

At least that particular aspect of public relations is down to me. At the British Grand Prix, the journalists who cover Formula One all season long have to go into overdrive to cope with the sudden demands of their editors to come up with a bit of sensation. The job they have to do is always the same – go out and find a powerful story that involves the British drivers. Like us, they are under pressure to deliver. We might be the subject of the stories they write, but we normally don't have a say about the content.

"I don't really like to think of myself as someone 'famous'."

Reading newspaper stories about yourself can often be a rather unsettling experience. It feels as if somebody else is at the tiller, as if your career path is being redirected without your control or involvement. This year's Silverstone Special was a good example. A story seemed to crop up in all the papers suggesting that I was on the point of retiring from Formula One. It was a good story, with one problem – it wasn't true.

A few years ago, I would have been quite upset by it, and I can still show a bit of temper if I think a journalist is being deliberately misleading, but, after a while, you start to realise that these stories have a very short life and they are part of the sport's image. By and large, I get on pretty well with the British Press pack, because I know that just as quickly as these stories appear, so they die away. Motor racing moves along at a heck of a pace and one good result will put things back into your control, and give the journalist something else to write about. In any case, there is a much larger picture for a driver to take into account than the one that appears in the paper, one that involves contracts, careers, engines, designers, sponsors and a whole host of other factors that go beyond a big headline.

Whatever might appear in the press, most of the supporters in the grandstand want to know only one thing about me – whether I am going to be in a position to win or not. The bottom line at Silverstone was that I wasn't.

Despite all the attention that comes with my job, I don't really like to think of myself as someone 'famous'. Still, fame is a fact that I can now enjoy, even if sometimes the interest crosses over into territory that I regard as private. I don't think it has changed me very much as a person. I have learnt a great deal and had some fascinating experiences, but I have the same personality and I still try to apply the same logic to what I do and the way I handle myself.

I have been through the mill a few times over the years, though, and had to keep on my toes. When I first broke into Formula One, I developed a defence mechanism to project the sort of person that I thought I should be, because I was not sure how to deal with the delicate politics of the sport. If I didn't know what to say or do, I did what I imagined to be appropriate and some of my comments from that era probably sounded a bit stilted and unnatural, which is exactly what they were. It wasn't because I was nervous about racing a Grand Prix car; I was just a little anxious about all the other trappings that come with being a Formula One racing driver at the front of the grid.

Getting my own back

**Waves of
support**

My father had a fantastic gift for putting people at their ease. He enjoyed his celebrity, probably rather more than I do. Whereas I am quite suspicious of fame, and of the speed at which a hero can suddenly be brought back down to earth, he revelled in people knowing who he was.

Fame was probably a great experience in the 1960s, when so many changes were taking place and the mood of the country was pretty good. It offered him a licence to enjoy himself and to meet a lot of interesting people and, because he had not grown up with a famous parent in the way that I did, it was a completely new experience for him. From my perspective, the fact that I grew up with that sort of backdrop meant that the simple act of being well known was never going to be enough to satisfy my ambitions.

Besides, the growing pots of money involved in Formula One, and in many other sports, mean that a driver's role has changed now. You have more responsibility to the sponsors, who tend to use drivers prominently in their marketing campaigns, and there is a far more prevalent air of political correctness hanging over sport today. The playboy outlook of the 1960s has been replaced with a far more corporate, clean-cut atmosphere, and the ever-growing media interest in motor racing means that drivers, like actors and politicians, are scrutinised far more than ever. Everything you say and do seems to be reported and commented on. There is less time off.

These days, I am more experienced at dealing with problems and situations and that means I can put more of the real me into what I do. I don't worry so much and I am a good deal more confident in dealing with the challenges that come my way. I might not relish them all, but I know now how to cope with just about everything that comes my way.

Thanks to my father, I was able to observe fame and its effects before I became well known myself. It was valuable and useful to have observed the way he handled fame and, because I was neither the famous person nor the fan, I could afford to sit back and learn.

On balance, the positive aspects of fame outweigh the negative. My public image may not tell the whole story of Damon Hill, but it is not a bad thing to be recognised and known for having done something positive and successful.

Press here

'Damon, give us a sign'

Thanks

In some ways, celebrity gives you a head start, a status that can sometimes make you feel as if you live in a small village. Some people whom I have never met are so used to seeing my face and hearing my voice on television and radio that think they know me, which is far nicer than anonymity. A few years ago, I might have gone into a petrol station or a corner shop and been greeted with a grunt by the guy behind the till, but now people are more welcoming and genuinely pleased to see me. I can have a quick chat while I get my change and then be on my way with a cheery goodbye, as if I visited that shop every day of the week.

Most people are great, but there are rare instances when you meet someone who sees himself as more important than anybody else and who will trample on small children in the effort to get his autograph book signed. And then there was the man who beat them all by nearly ruining my perfect day . . .

In 1994 I won the British Grand Prix, the culmination of a long-cherished dream. It had been an exhilarating occasion, all the more so since my father had never won the event, and I was elated. Afterwards, I was enjoying myself, celebrating with some friends, and we were besieged by autograph hunters in the Silverstone paddock as the evening drew in. For once, I had the time to sign everybody's books and, after a day like the one I had had, I was happy to do so.

'It's been a fantas-
tic day – let's not
spoil it.'

Focal point

As I was signing away, I was cornered by one man who became quite insistent that I should leave everything else and come to meet his friends, who were waiting in another part of the circuit. I said no, as politely as I could, but he didn't seem to take that for an answer, and continued to pressure me into trailing along behind him to some distant corner of Silverstone. I began to get a little annoyed and told him very firmly that I was quite happy where I was, I didn't have the time to go and meet his mates, so please could he go away and leave me in peace. At that point he looked me straight in the eye and said, 'Look, we're all a bit tired, it's been a fantastic day – let's not spoil it.' I had just won my home Grand Prix, and he was advising me not to ruin my day! Classic.

You can never please everybody. Whatever you do or say in life, there will always be somebody out there who holds the opposite opinion. I sometimes feel that I am walking on eggshells when I am in the public eye because I end up worrying that things I say and do might be misconstrued. It is easy to offend people or to disappoint them, but equally you don't want to go round with a cheesy grin on your face all the time. Life for a racing driver is something of a balancing act, both on the track and off it.

In the paddock as well, I have to be careful what I say. With the amount of media attention that the sport attracts, the days have pretty much gone when a driver can fire off indiscriminately on any subject that takes his fancy. There

150

My newest fan

**Behind every
'great' (!?) man . . .**

are so many groups of people who have a major influence on a team, be they engine suppliers, sponsors or any of the other companies who support us over a season, that you cannot really say what you think all the time, for fear of seriously offending the very people who help to get your car on the track in the first place. You have to weigh up the desire to be completely honest in your interviews against the damage that such bluntness can do.

That's why you hear so many drivers giving cautious answers, talking about the 'room for improvement' in their engines, or the 'encouraging signals' from the team. We all end up becoming masters of the euphemism and, if you are not careful, that can stifle your natural character. As soon as that happens, the world jumps on your back and accuses you of lacking personality. Sometimes you might as well sit back phlegmatically and accept that you can never win.

It is a battle that most of us were not prepared for. Drivers come into Formula One because they want to race on the biggest stage, not because they crave some sort of stardom. You are used to having an audience for what you do, from your days in the junior formulae, but actually having a group of devoted fans who follow your career and actively support you above anybody else is not something that many drivers bank on. Suddenly you have to deal with autographs, interviews, fan mail and attention when you go to the supermarket or arrive at an airport, and it all comes as something of a surprise, unless, like a growing number of the young drivers now coming in, you started working on your image long before you ever got into a Grand Prix car.

> "Drivers come into Formula One because they want to race on the biggest stage."

One of the problems is that fame hits you hard only when you get to Formula One. The well-established career pattern of golfers, footballers or athletes, for example, allows the public to get to know them and they get used to being in the spotlight. In motor racing, even though Formula 3000 and Formula 3 races get decent-sized crowds, the wider world has very little knowledge of your career until you climb into the seat of a Grand Prix car. Until then, in the opinion of almost everybody, you might as well have not existed.

Even within Formula One, there are different levels of celebrity. There is a great deal of difference between the attention that drivers get by participating in the sport and the focus that falls on them when they are in the position to win races. Then there is the attention that goes the way of whichever drivers are fighting for that year's world championship. When you are in that position, the scrutiny is absolutely remorseless. Everywhere you go, people want their pound of flesh and, at a time when you need to be concentrating as much as possible on doing your job, you find yourself thrown under the microscope like an insect on a slide. After a while, it can all become a little bit oppressive.

The brunt of fame landed on my shoulders when I started racing for Williams. The intensity was more than I had ever expected and I felt that I needed to do something quickly

to justify the amount of coverage I was receiving. I had been racing for only a short period, but my picture seemed to be in the papers all the time and, rather than boosting my ego, it actually piled the pressure on me. I was aware of the disparity between my profile and my results, but there seemed to be nothing I could do about it.

Any young driver who gets his break with a big team has that problem. It is a bit like being the manager of the England football team – you have to do something so your performances can be fairly analysed, but long before you ever get the chance, you are judged and dissected.

It took time, but I have now learnt to deal with that attention and even enjoy it. A lot of that peace of mind comes down to the fact that, in the end, I did produce the displays that I needed to win over most of the critics and close that

Happiness is home

gap between prominence and performance. I have had more than twenty race victories, and a world championship, and that is a record that always has to be taken into consideration, even by my critics.

Mind you, one look at the papers after some of my problems earlier this season put a damper on that particular brand of confidence. In Formula One, you are frequently seen as being only as good as your last race, which certainly wasn't working in my favour after the British Grand Prix. I spun off, the first person to retire from the race, and found myself in an even worse position than in the previous season, when I had one point after Silverstone. Now I had none, and I wanted to get away from motor racing for a couple of days to minimise the disappointment.

When I am not driving, I like to be at home, with the doors closed, and spend time with my family. Racing drivers belong to a privileged profession, well paid and well known, but I think we still have the right to set aside a part of our lives for ourselves, our family and friends. If you want to remain sane, you cannot spend your whole life being a racing driver.

At home, I can relax and turn off, do something else and leave racing cars behind for a little while. Like most other people, I like to have some time when I don't think about my job and, even if it is very different from most people's, it is still a job. I like to take an interest in whatever my children are doing, but I would be absolutely horrified if I were to get home and find them quizzing me about motor racing for hour after hour. The good news is that it hasn't happened – yet.

Time out

"Fame, though, can be transitory and it can be inconstant, and I have learnt to value my privacy."

My sort of fame has been an education, as you see all sides of human nature. I have witnessed great generosity, and equally I have seen some acts of extreme greed, and I have learnt the precious lesson of distinguishing between those two. Fame can be transitory and it can be inconstant, and I have learnt to value my privacy. I don't want to hide things from people or be aloof, because my supporters have been very important to me over the years, but there are certain things, such as the time I spend with my family, that I do not want to trade for fame.

One thing I love is getting home and being treated like nobody special. If I'm not a useful member of our family, then I get no respect either from Georgie or from my children. There's no VIP treatment in our house, and that's the most 'real' experience of life that I have, and I would be lost without it. At the track, everything is triumph and disaster; at home, they are not allowed to be impostors.

Everybody is in Formula One to win. It's the pinnacle of ambition, the goal that all the teams and drivers work towards, the inspiration for all the graft. Even if you are struggling along at the back of the grid with a team that has no money and no realistic chance of getting into the points, hope still springs eternal. With luck, some money and talented people, every team has the potential to get to the front. For the driver, it's a case of being good enough, being in the right place and believing in yourself. At Spa, all my hopes came together, and this is the story of that weekend.

I was lucky to start off my Formula One career with Williams, a team who know all about winning. They set a remarkable standard of achievement and if anybody questions that quality, all Frank and Patrick have to do is open the books and show off the role call of championships and victories. That kind of success does not come easily and it rubs off on the people around them. If you look at their mechanics' faces after they have had a bad weekend, you can see their disappointment.

Williams appreciate that every little bit matters, whether it is the car, the mechanics, the team management or the driver. Every part of the process needs to be in place before you can start a race weekend with the real ambition of ending it on top of the podium, and that is the lesson I took with me when I left the team. Whatever else may have happened, I will always be grateful to them for teaching me that.

In addition, I was team-mate to Alain Prost, Ayrton Senna and Nigel Mansell, fantastically successful drivers who each had their own way of going about things. Alain and Ayrton, in particular, were perfectionists who would go to any length to get what they wanted. My father, who was a stickler for getting things right, was another driver who fell into that category.

The lesson was clear – you cannot be satisfied if something has been left half done. If there is the smallest improvement that can be made, you have to go for it. If 100 per cent is achievable, you can't be happy with 99 per cent.

That sort of coaching becomes ingrained. You think about winning rather than finishing, of championships rather than near-misses, and you get a high from that confidence. It is a great feeling being in the lead in a Grand Prix and, after I had left Williams, leading in Hungary at the wheel of an Arrows was a fantastic experience. It reminded me how much I missed the high that only winners get. It also made me hungry to rediscover that feeling of pure delight that comes from victory.

An early influence – Patrick Head

One of the main reasons that Eddie had been so keen to sign me was for that experience of being at the front, of having won races and dealt with the pressure. Almost immediately I had signed, the team wanted me to tell them what they should do to help Benson and Hedges Jordan turn into winners, perhaps to let them into some of the secrets I had picked up from Williams. The trouble was that there was no panacea, no bit of magic that would get Jordan there. It was a question of doing the same tasks, but doing them better and doing them consistently. My contribution was to impress upon everyone what a big difference a lot of small things can make. Put them together, and they can be the difference between coming second and first.

Initially, I think they were disappointed that I was telling them things they already knew. When you have worked in Formula One for years, aspiring to win but never quite getting there, it is easy to imagine that there is another planet that the winners and champions inhabit, so when I

moved to Jordan, there was a bit of curiosity about how I might do things. They wanted to know what was so different about a world champion and they wondered if I would be an instant fix, or if I could provide a list of do's and don'ts that would put us on the pace from day one.

Instead, all I could suggest was that they should continue to do the same job, but to do it better, and that probably came as something of a disappointment. I suppose it was the equivalent of someone saying to me: 'If you want to win again, why don't you just drive faster and try to beat the guy in front?' My answer would have been 'Don't you think I know that?' and maybe theirs was the same. As much as I needed to push them in one direction, I also needed to convince and encourage the team that it was the basics that counted.

The difficulty was that there was such an enormous gulf between where we were at the start of the year and where we needed to be to challenge for a win or two, so a lot of what I was saying was redundant. At the start of the season, we were not looking for the last per cent – we were looking for just about the whole thing, and it took time to find. The fact that we managed to do it at all is remarkable.

After the disaster of Monaco, our performances improved gradually, and Spa was our next destination. We had been starting to qualify well and were coming close to getting a place on the podium. Ralf and I both did well in the previous two races, in Hockenheim and Hungary, and finished in the points, so we came to Spa in pretty good spirits. A victory did not look likely, but a decent performance did.

Ayrton Senna – dedicated to winning

A sweet and sour year for Gary Anderson

Spa has always been a good race for Jordan. They nearly won it with Andrea de Cesaris, Michael Schumacher qualified seventh there in his first-ever race – before being poached by Benetton – and Rubens Barrichello gave Jordan their one and only pole position when he took advantage of a damp Belgian qualifying session. Everyone in the team was looking forward to Spa, including me.

I expected Spa to be a very competitive contest. Michael Schumacher and Mika Hakkinen were fighting hard for the world championship title, and Michael is a Spa specialist as he grew up not far from the circuit. It was going to be extremely tough to join their battle, but we all had a very good feeling about the race and were looking forward to the weekend.

My only slip at Spa

The warm-up sessions went extremely well, and I managed to get the car set up nicely, so we went into qualifying with a strong degree of optimism. Drivers have a limit of twelve laps for the one hour of qualifying, which always starts on the dot of 1 p.m. This actually means we have a choice of the normal four runs of one complete timed lap (because we have to use up two laps on each run, going out and coming into the pits) or any other permutation, provided we do not exceed the limit of twelve laps. Around Spa, a long circuit with demanding corners and fast straights, the tyres were past their best after one timed lap, so the best tactic was to take four cracks at getting the perfect lap. That is a lot of concentrated effort.

For a long while I stood third on the timing screen behind the two McLarens, but then, not long after I had finished my third run, I was bumped back a place by Schumacher. I was temporarily frustrated by that, but more determined than ever to pull out something special for the final run. I could see that there was not a lot between us and I was certain that I would improve my time, but the question was whether he would do the same.

We all waited. This was the big crunch. Would Michael get pole position? Would I get my place back? I made my decision to leave the garage with two and a half minutes to go. You have to start your last lap before the one hour session is up, but if you manage to do that, then your time still counts. As long as you cross the line to start the timed lap before the red light comes on, then you're okay. In those circumstances, I wanted to leave it as late as possible to get as clear a run as I could.

I wasn't the only one who planned it that way. As I came out of my garage, I saw Hakkinen, Coulthard and then Schumacher emerging just ahead of me – a train of cars all fighting it out for the top four places. As we set off, Michael started to back off on the throttle, giving the McLarens time to get away so they didn't hold him up when he was on a quick lap. The trouble was that I didn't want to be held up by him either, nor did I want to overtake him, because my plan was to be the last guy setting his qualifying time. Instead, for half a lap, I stuck closely to the rear of Michael's car until it was clear that we would both get across the start line in time. After that, I backed off to give myself some space and concentrated on trying to do one perfect lap.

I could see Michael in front of me when we both started our quickest laps. There are a couple of points on the circuit where you can judge the distance between yourself and the car in front, and halfway around I could see that I had

"I was third on the grid and the car was quick. Could I win?"

closed the gap. That meant one thing – my lap was going better than his, a piece of good news just when I needed it. For the last half of the lap I gave it everything and in the last section of the circuit I made up a lot of time. I knew it had been a good lap, certainly my best so far, but I didn't know how good Michael's had been. He might have improved over the second half, for instance, and there was no point in celebrating only to find that I was still behind the Ferrari.

In fact, I didn't have to wait long. As I started to coast home, Dino, my engineer, came on the radio and said, 'Well done, Damon. You're third.' That single moment was the best point of my season, and it sparked off one thought straight away – I was third on the grid and the car was quick. Could I win?

I went into a press conference afterwards and said that I wasn't thinking about the race and that I was just happy to be third on the grid. Of course, that wasn't really true, because the taste for victory had returned and I had no intention of frittering away the opportunity. The McLarens looked quick, but we didn't expect them to be so fast in race trim, and we had had the powerful fillip of beating Schumacher at his favourite circuit. Once I was back from the conference, I was quite happy to settle down to

pondering our race strategy, calculating the possibilities and poring over the data. When you're stuck down the grid, it can be a laborious process, but this time I went to it with a lot of gusto. A sniff of victory gives everybody a burst of energy.

There is a difference between wanting to win and being a dreamer, a difference between doing whatever it takes to come home first and being unrealistic. If you qualified tenth because you were consistently 1.5 seconds off the pace, then it's unrealistic to come up with a race strategy intended to win the race. This time, though, we knew we had a chance of beating McLaren in a straight fight if the tyres gave us an advantage or if we came up with a better race strategy.

New recruit Mike Gascoyne plans for the future

The expectation changed the complexion of our normal pre-race briefing and, for me, it was very much an old, familiar feeling. There would not have been too much difference between the atmosphere of preparation in the meeting

room inside the B & H Jordan truck that Saturday night and the same room in the Williams truck during the years I raced for them. It is a mind game peppered with strategy, very much akin to a military campaign, where you all sit down to bash out the different permutations, prepare for the race and try to guess what the other teams are going to do.

It is a matter of educated guesswork where, like a spy trailing his opposite number, you try to put yourself in somebody else's position and work out what move they are going to make. 'What would I do in Hakkinen's shoes? What about Schumacher? What are they going to get Eddie

Irvine to do this time?' Like chess, you are thinking and second guessing in the safe knowledge that everybody else is doing the same thing. The crucial question is often not what your team is going to do, but what people will expect you to do.

At Spa, there is one other factor that you cannot ignore – a climate that no weatherman can ever get to grips with. Our forecast on Saturday evening had predicted only a very slight chance of rain for the race, but sure enough the sky was slate grey when we woke up and it started to drizzle in the morning, prompting the usual comments that this would play into Michael's hands.

Working closely with my race engineer, Dino Toso

Despite the hype, I was quite happy to see the rain falling. Goodyear's wet weather tyre was very good, which was a possible advantage over the McLarens, and I don't mind driving in the wet. I have participated in enough races not to be out-psyched by pre-race predictions regarding the prowess of others, and I wasn't going to be handing this race to anybody without a fight, whatever the conditions.

As we got to the grid, it was clear that the rain was getting heavier and, having done my lap to the grid on intermediate tyres that are only suitable for a damp track, I knew I wouldn't be able to use them without losing places or aquaplaning off. There was no choice for me – it had to be wet weather tyres.

Nearly without exception, everyone started the race on full wet tyres. It was quite wet then, but, as suddenly as it had started, the rain stopped soon after. Looking back, the best option would have been to have started on intermediates – which was exactly what Schumacher had done. How did he know what the weather was going to do? At the second start, he was on a full downforce, wet weather set-up, even though it had stopped raining. So what happened? It began to rain again and he had his car in the right configuration once more. At Spa, he can be infuriatingly good at predicting the weather!

The first start was dreadful. I slipped the clutch too hard and then had to pull it in as it grabbed. By the time I had engaged it again, I had ruined my start and lost a lot of time. I think I was sixth in the first turn, and in a grandstand seat to see the early stages of the thirteen-car pile-up at the first corner. Coulthard and Irvine were being pushy and apparently made contact, then David escaped ahead of me. I found some traction and raced off towards the awesome rise through Eau Rouge, but David didn't make it. He seemed to hit a bump, which threw his car to the right and straight into the concrete wall. I was immediately behind him and knew what to expect next, but not what to do about it. It was one of those split-second decisions which make so much difference to one's day. Knowing that he would rebound, I could hit the brakes and run the risk of the rest of the pack piling into me, or I could just keep my foot down and hope for the best.

Thankfully, one of his detached wheels helped me make up my mind. It flew towards me and I realised that if I didn't brake I would catch it. As soon as that and the rest of David's wreckage had passed within inches of the front of my car, I jumped back on the gas and got out. I knew, however, that there would be a big shunt behind me.

Chasing the title – Michael and Mika

I expected the safety car to come out, but I was a little surprised to see the red flags that meant the race was being stopped. Charlie Whiting, the race director, had a meeting with the drivers before the race and told us to expect the safety car to emerge if there was a first-lap accident because he didn't want to have to restart. His plan was obviously aimed at stopping any risky business at the first corner, because a driver who crashes out in the early stages doesn't get a second chance if the safety car is called into action, but he does if there is a red flag. Charlie's logic was quite sensible, but he could have had no idea that the first-lap accident he had predicted would turn out to be such an enormous smash, with wrecked

cars everywhere. In those circumstances, he had no choice but to stop the race – if he hadn't, we might have had trouble racing our way around salvage trucks for an hour and a half.

At the time, I didn't know the sheer scale of the crash. I came round again and parked on the grid and from there, around the corner from the chaos, you couldn't see anything. I was expecting a five- or ten-minute delay at most, so, while other people were getting out of their cars and wandering off, I decided to sit tight. Dino told me there would be a big delay, but I stayed put and, fifty minutes later, I was still there. All the while, I was getting myself

Slip sliding away

psyched up, running over the mistakes I had made at the first start and getting myself motivated so that I wouldn't make the same errors the next time. While everyone else was lining up, I was more concerned about staying calm than feeling motivated.

The weather, as usual, played its hand. While they were clearing away the crash, the sun emerged, so we had to make a new plan based on using intermediate tyres and a different set-up. I didn't want to be conservative, so I reduced the amount of wing we used, something that other people on the grid were not doing. As long as it continued to dry out, I knew I would be sitting pretty. At the time, it seemed to me that the weather had turned.

Reducing wing means changing the angle of the front and rear wings to cut the downforce holding the car to the track. In tricky conditions, you normally try to have as much downforce as you can to stop the car floating and then aquaplaning, but the problem is that the more downforce you use, the slower the car is on the straights. Taking off wing meant the car would be more difficult to handle as long as the track was wet, but when it dried I would have more speed than most. It was a gamble, a case of everything or nothing, and on another day it could have backfired miserably. Spa, though, turned out to be our race.

Your decision as to whether or not to take a risk like that is affected by a lot of things, including confidence,

168

Spa – always begs
the question wet
or dry

Difficult decisions

ambition, the state of the championship and your own fear of failure. Hakkinen, for instance, would have been unwise to have gambled in the way that I did because he had a championship lead to protect, while Schumacher could take risks because coming second was no use to him then.

For me, the second start was a reprieve, because I had screwed up the first one, and I was not intending to repeat that failure. Lo and behold, I didn't. I made an absolutely perfect start and outbraked Hakkinen into the first corner. After that, Mika tangled with Schumacher and put himself out of the race. That was one rival out of the way even before we'd done 400 yards and David Coulthard spun off the track not much later. David, of course, managed to keep going and, although he was out of contention for a win, his part in the drama was a long way from over.

On the opening laps, I was able to draw out a lead and things were looking good. The car felt comfortable, I was driving well and a drier racing line had begun to emerge, a fact that suited my car's set-up to a tee. Everything was beginning to play right into my hands – and that was when the rain started to fall again.

At Spa it customarily rains in some parts of the circuit and not in others, and this time it was raining by the pits and at Stavelot. First it was light, then it got much heavier and soon it was clear that the intermediates were not able to cope with the rain in those areas.

Schumacher caught up and started to harry me. He was running with more downforce than me, which is why I was prospering while it stayed dry and I could drive hard. Once

"All of a sudden, Eddie was looking at a double-podium finish."

the rain started, I had to tiptoe around and avoid aqua-planing off the track, but Michael could brake later and accelerate harder. Once he had caught me up, it was just a question of time before he passed, and if I had put up a strong fight, it would probably have ended with me spinning out. Much as I was sorry to lose the lead, I had to let Michael go.

I had raced at Spa before when the weather had brightened as quickly as it had rained, and if that happened, I knew I would be in a good position again. My optimistic side was telling me to hang on and get back at Michael when the weather changed. The pessimistic side of me, though, was thinking that the race was beginning to look like another Michael Schumacher Spa domination show.

In Belgium, he seems to have some kind of control over the weather, as if he has his hand clenched around the top of a mighty tap somewhere. Just when he needed rain, it appeared, tumbling from the sky more and more ferociously. The rain had stopped for fifty minutes before the restart and I had gambled on the basis of that. At the same time, sitting on the grid alongside me, with the sun beginning to appear and the track drying, Michael had chosen to set his car up for the sort of heavy rain showers that didn't seem possible, but, of course, that was exactly what appeared. If he ever gets bored of racing, I'm sure Michael would do a great job as a weather forecaster.

By now, my tyres were all but useless. Intermediates don't have the deep grooves you need to displace water. On a damp track they are fine, but with standing water they can't cope. When I came in for my first pit-stop, it was obvious that we had to change to wets, and that meant adjusting the front wing as well to alter the aerodynamic balance of the car. We had a bit of a problem, because the mechanic could not get the spanner out of the wing adjuster, but Jim Vale, the team manager, did the decent thing by pulling back sharply on the mechanic, which pulled the spanner out at the same time. In the midst of all the action, there was no time to see the funny side.

I got out of the pits, but Michael was 15 seconds in the lead and I was having to focus on the obvious objective of staying on the track, while trying to push as hard as I could. Ralf, like his brother, had gambled on having more wing than me, and he had fought his way up to third place, a terrific performance from a guy who had such a wild reputation at the start of the season. All of a sudden, Eddie was looking at a double-podium finish.

Any victory owes something to fortune and to the outcome of a few, crucial episodes. When the luck is with you, they go your way and you benefit accordingly. When your luck is out, you end up in a gravel trap or you trundle back to the pits with a mechanical failure, bemoaning your bad fortune. It's the same for every driver and every team and,

The great escape

The start of something big

on that wet day, two things happened within a few minutes of each other that put us on the road to victory.

First, I hit another car, but kept going. Then, Michael did the same thing, albeit with a great deal more force, and knocked himself out of the race. From those two acorns sprung my first win for two seasons, and Jordan's first victory ever.

The visibility during the race was terrible, but I had to keep pushing to stay ahead of Ralf and to try to catch Michael. I came up to lap Jarno Trulli's Prost and, as I went to pass, saw him moving across in my direction. Even when I was completely alongside, he still didn't see me because of

the spray, and the first that he knew about it was when my left front wheel hit his right front.

It was a big moment. On a bad day, my wheel could have snapped off or I could have ridden over his tyre and gone airborne. Instead, we just bounced off each other and kept on going. It was a close call, but I thought I had got cleanly away and it was the last I saw of Trulli.

In fact, the collision had broken the rim on the left rear wheel. I wasn't aware that wheel had hit him, but somewhere along the line it must have done. I didn't realise what the problem was, but air was leaking from the tyre, dropping the pressure and slowing me down. The damage

was only discovered when they changed the tyres at the next pit-stop, and gave the old wheels a once-over. By all accounts, the wheel wouldn't have lasted more than another two or three laps. Trulli, by the way, didn't know that it was me whom he had hit until I spoke to him about it at Monza the following week. He thought it had been a Tyrrell, which meant he never even saw the blinding yellow of our B & H livery!

Then came Michael's infamous collision with David Coulthard. I was still running second when, out of the blue, Dino told me over the radio that Schumacher was out of the race. Normally if someone has had a crash, you see their car by the side of the circuit as confirmation of the news, but there was no sign of his Ferrari. It is unusual to have a crash that puts you out of the race, but which still allows you to drive back to the pits, so I was mildly intrigued, but there wasn't time to ask any more. I knew only that Michael was out and I was leading the race.

The point at which you discover you are in the lead of a race is the moment that defines your ability to withstand pressure. Some people revel in it, others find it all too much and wilt under the burden. For me, it is a familiar, exciting feeling that I have grown used to in my career. It spurs me on to concentrate harder and nurture the car, to make the most of an opportunity.

Over the years I have had lots of experience being in front and, now that the chance had come again, I was enjoying it. All the while, the thought was going through my mind that this could be Jordan's first win, and I could imagine the combination of fear and excitement that Eddie must

Not to be for Mika

have been feeling. I had started the season wanting to be the first guy to win a race for his team; now I had the chance, I was not going to let it slip through my fingers.

There was still no time for complacency. Giancarlo Fisichella, the man who nearly won this race for Jordan last year, came to the fore again, but this time for all the wrong reasons. With visibility now virtually nil, he slammed into the back of Shinji Nakano's Minardi at the Bus Stop chicane, spraying pieces of bodywork all over the track and giving himself a nasty fright into the bargain by ripping apart a considerable amount of his Benetton. The safety car came out immediately, and that was the moment when it could have all gone wrong for me, because Ralf had already made his pit-stop and I hadn't. When the safety car comes out, the field bunches up behind it, reducing wide leads to

Nearly home . . . but not dry

almost nothing. The 15-second lead that I had enjoyed over Ralf was imminently going to be cut, so I had to make my stop there and then and hope I could still come out ahead of Ralf. I did.

Now Ralf was on my tail and, at the same time, my wife was on the phone to Michael Breen, my lawyer, asking him to plead with somebody to get the race stopped, because she had seen enough. She was on holiday in Spain and by this point she was a nervous wreck, not because I was winning, but because of all the accidents.

After a few laps behind the safety car, I thought they should stop it too. The race was nearly over and we were running out of both cars and time, but this being Formula One, I

guess all the drama was simply adding to the show. Whatever the drivers might have thought, there was no way they would call an early halt to such an incident-packed race, so I started to think about what would happen when the safety car went in and, with Ralf directly behind me, there were some decisions to be made.

"The race was nearly over and we were running out of both cars and time . . ."

My fear was that Ralf, who was suing Jordan for the right to leave for Williams, would feel under no obligation to obey team orders. With only ten laps to go, he might see this as a chance to win, and if he tried to overtake me at the restart, we could both end up in the gravel.

It was a risk for the team and, of course, there was also the selfish aspect that I had already lost my 15-second lead because of the safety car, and I didn't want to lose out to Ralf in the race because of that. I got on the radio to my engineers and said, 'Tell Eddie that it's up to him. We can race for this, and there will be a chance that neither of us will finish, or he can tell Ralf to hold station and that way we stand a good chance of getting a 1–2. It's up to Eddie.'

I didn't want it to come across as something I was demanding or needed to have happen (I have my pride still!) so I emphasised that the decision was down to the team, and to Eddie in particular. It was obvious how much both of us wanted to win, and that we would fight for victory against anybody, including our own team-mate. When the decision came, it was to tell Ralf to back off. I was relieved, but not completely convinced that he would accept it, so when the safety car went in and we started racing again, I legged it into the first corner.

It was just as well, because Ralf was pushing hard. He had to, because Alesi, in third place, was breathing down his neck, but I didn't want to give Ralf a tempting sight of the lead and then suffer the consequences. To the viewer, it might have looked like we were coming home in formation, but, believe me, we were racing the last ten laps and

I feel confident that even if Ralf had tried to get past me, he would not have managed it.

As I crossed the line, I was elated – for Eddie, for the team and, a little, for myself. This was my first win in a car other than a Williams and there have been very few drivers who have gone from one team to another and continued to win. I felt proud that I had led a race in an Arrows, where I nearly won, and now I had won a race in a Jordan. When I was at Williams, I was always told that I was lucky to have the best car in the field, which cast a shadow over my ability. Winning at Spa proved that there has always been more to it than just driving the best car.

Fizzy's crash sends out the safety car

**Cracked it –
Eddie Jordan
on the podium**

I knew I had driven well all weekend, and the reward came from the sea of smiling faces that beamed up at me when I was on the podium. As luck would have it, Eddie had organised a coachload of people from the factory to come out to the race, and there they all were, cheering and, in some cases, crying with the emotion of it. The luck had gone our way, and now we had half the workforce ready to celebrate – and, believe me, they did.

I went out to win that race. Rain is a great leveller, but we took full advantage of the conditions, which were the same for everybody, and made the most of our opportunity. For the B & H Jordan Mugen-Honda team, it had been a tremendous race weekend, one that elevated us into the racewinners' circle and demonstrated that victory is an attainable target. We were within touching distance of third place in the constructors' championship and, after the start to the year that we had had, the idea of beating both Williams and Benetton was almost too much to believe.

I was a very happy man when I finally managed to find a way out of the circuit that evening. Behind me, the party was still going strong, but I wanted to get home and celebrate with my family. Not many drivers have won with different teams and, without taking anything away from Eddie, the Jordan was still not the best in the field, but we had come home first and second in the season's toughest race. It had been a while coming, but I, and all of the B & H Jordan team, had proved a point. Together we had cracked it.

Quite pleased

There is a special feeling about the Italian Grand Prix at Monza. It is not just the fans and the history that makes it unique, but also the circuit itself – a long, sweeping series of straights with a few corners thrown in for good measure.

At Monza we reach a speed of around 220mph at the end of the main straight and we don't hit the brakes until there are 150 metres to the corner, yet we can still scrub off enough of that momentum to get round the corner, lap after lap. If you want an example of just how powerful the brakes are on a Formula One car, there you have it.

By the time you do finally go for the brakes, the car has already stopped accelerating, because Monza is the one place where our cars reach maximum speed and those 150 metres disappear very quickly. It is like starting up the motorway slip road at more than three times the speed limit, braking halfway along and still expecting to get round the roundabout at the end.

At 220mph, you are pressed tight against the seatbelt straps thanks to pure speed. You are being pushed back in your seat, foot flat on the gas, waiting, waiting and then – bang – 150 metres before the corner, you have to stamp on the brake so hard that you end the race with a dead foot. As your speed falls away, you are thrown forward, tensing yourself once more against the straps as, all the while, you are thrown around by the bumps. The car

might look big and strong on the television screen, but remember that the whole machine only weighs 600 kilos, which is less than the weight of a rugby scrum. When you think that a good deal of that weight is taken up by a big engine and racing tyres, it's not surprising that the car goes so quickly.

Late braking is one of the arts of Formula One, a discipline that takes time to come to terms with. Plenty get it wrong, but when the car is right, it can be one of the most exciting parts of driving.

If a Formula One driver worried all the time about danger, he would be doing the wrong job. Invariably the enjoyment of racing far outweighs any trepidation. Fear is shoved aside as a totally redundant state of mind and from there you largely forget about it.

It would do you no good to occupy your thoughts with concerns about your speed or your chances of being injured. In fact, those sorts of worries would put you in more danger, because your concentration would be affected and you would be more susceptible to making errors. Drivers find it harder to go slowly than to push themselves to the extreme. If they try to stay within some kind of safe limit, they tend to seize up and lose their natural style, which is when mistakes creep in. The irony is that a frightened, nervous driver trying to stay out of trouble would probably be the most dangerous guy on the track.

A driver has to have faith in the equipment and in him-self. You couldn't race if you didn't have that basic level of confidence and self-belief, that certain knowledge that, whatever gets thrown in your direction on the track, you will be able to cope. As a driver, you have to believe that you are in control of the experience and that what happens is down to you. As long as you continue to believe in your-self, you are well equipped for Formula One.

Our quest does not stem from some macho need to show off. The goal in our sport is simply to beat the other guys on the track in a straight race run according to rules that we all know and, as such, I don't hold with the descrip-tion of racing drivers as being brave. I would define bravery as doing something unselfish or risking your life for the benefit of others, whereas motor racing has a far more selfish streak running through it. It's a personal challenge, a thrill and a discipline, a useful skill to learn, but is it brave? I don't think so.

The nearest we come to bravery are those occasions when a driver has to confront trepidation to get the most from his car. At somewhere like Eau Rouge, the soaring curve at the end of Spa's main straight, it can take a bit of convincing from the cockpit that you really can go flat out, but it is that sort of challenge that keeps you motivated, because we all develop a desire to push ourselves to the limit and to prove the doubter wrong. If people say Eau Rouge can't be done flat, then you can bet that every driver will give it a go at some point over the weekend, just to see if he can prove otherwise. The anxiety that haunts a

Goodwood – good fun

Over the summer, during a break from Formula One, I drove a couple of vintage cars at Goodwood and it was quite an eye-opening experience. The whole event was meticulously planned to recreate the feel of the 1950s and 1960s, and there were few concessions to modern safety standards. Better seatbelts had been fitted or, in the case of some of the cars, belts were fitted for the first time, and the drivers were allowed to use full-face crash helmets, but otherwise the cars were unchanged from the standards of the day, an era when drivers had a much shorter life expectancy behind the wheel.

They might not have had the performance of today's Formula One cars, but to have sat in those machines and raced round the old Nurburgring, a circuit going on for nearly 14 miles without run-off areas, crash barriers or even the painted white line at the edge of the track, would have meant closing your mind to dangers that anybody could see. In those days, drivers were killed on a regular basis, but the sport went on, slowly learning its lessons.

driver does not come from fear of injury, but from a fear of falling short, of failing.

If I make any sort of mistake, I consider it to be costly to my performance. Losing control of my car during a Grand Prix will cost me a place or perhaps even the race itself, and the same principle is true in qualifying. I worry about crashing, but only for that reason. A crash means a bad place on the grid or no points from a race weekend, and that is a failure. Above all else, I try to drive the car as hard as I can, but you always need to deliver it back to the garage, ready to fight another day.

Mind you, we are lucky to be driving in an era when safety has become one of the sport's most pressing concerns.

I grew up in the full knowledge that my father raced with guys who, from time to time, were killed, so occasional deaths were part of the sport that I knew. For the past decade and a half, though, Formula One has been comparatively safe and a lot of people gradually forgot the danger that is implicit in motor racing, which is why the deaths of Ayrton Senna and Roland Ratzenberger at the San Marino Grand Prix in 1994 came as such a profound shock to so many people. Somebody like Rubens Barrichello, for instance, had been a small boy the last time a driver had been killed in a Grand Prix, and then, suddenly, two men died in a weekend.

The real 'old man'

The serious side

"There are times when you get out of the car and thank God that you got out of a race in one piece."

As Ayrton's team-mate, the accident obviously had potentially serious ramifications for me. We had been using identical equipment, but it never crossed my mind not to rejoin the race that afternoon. I had to go back on to the track for the same reasons that we had all decided to race on after Roland's accident. There was no decision to be made.

I had to trust what I was being told by my engineers and I took part in that race as an act of faith in their judgment. Without that bond, how could the sport ever go on? There are times when you get out of the car and thank God that you got out of a race in one piece, and Imola was one of them, but we are racing drivers and that is our job.

We all chose to do this in the first place and, whatever happens, you carry on and take your chance. Not to have gone back into that race because my team-mate had had such a dreadful accident would have been an act of hypocrisy on my part. You cannot take up a lifestyle such as this because of all the good things and then call an abrupt halt when something bad happens – even something as bad as that.

I remember Niki Lauda's comment about the Imola weekend because it was typically astute. He said God had had his hand over Formula One, but for that weekend he had decided to lift it off. Lauda was right – we had been lucky not to have had a fatality for twelve years and we have been lucky not to have had one since, but we would be wise to remember that one day it will happen again.

Still, there are a few drivers out there who have a poor understanding of the risks, and, in a way, perhaps it helps them. The ideal attitude for a racing driver is probably to believe that he will never be hurt, which is a necessary state of mind for men and women who have done dangerous jobs throughout history. Taking risks, though, is easy if you're not fully aware of the level of danger – if a cat knew how painful it would be to fall off a roof, then it might not go up there in the first place.

There are things you can do if you are ignorant of the dangers, and driving in the wet when you cannot see is, arguably, beyond risky and into the realms of plain stupidity, but someone like Ayrton was acutely aware of the dangers he faced, which made his performances all the more remarkable. Despite any reservations he may have had, he never let fear restrict his performance. As human beings, we admire people who know the depth of the risks they are taking, rather than those who are blissfully ignorant.

The other side

A lot of drivers remain complacent about danger, while just about all of us have a fatalistic view of accidents. If it's going to happen, then it will, and there is not a lot you can do about it – like fighter pilots, racing drivers are not normally the sort of people who want to go through life cocooned in cotton wool.

Jacques Villeneuve suggested that drivers are losing the admiration of the public because Formula One is becoming too safe, but surely people won't have respect for people who take absurd risks. I calculate the odds and I accept them, but I don't see any need to load them up against me. Statistics can tell you the chances of contracting a fatal disease, or getting hit by a car, or being struck by a meteorite or swept away by a tidal wave. If you took all of them into account, you would never leave your house. There is a risk to everything, and that includes motor racing, but the positives far outweigh the negatives. As long as motor racing offers me a level of challenge and enjoyment and a way of fulfilling my potential, then the deal is a good one.

Mind you, sometimes the risks come from unexpected sources. I had two near-misses within the space of five days in September. The first one came when I was flying home from the Nurburgring, after a rather disappointing time in the Luxembourg Grand Prix – a classic case of 'just when you thought it was safe to relax'.

I was in my jet with some friends and we took off from Cologne Airport as normal. As we were climbing, I heard the undercarriage being retracted and then dropped again. Shortly afterwards, I heard the wheels being brought up once more. I made some joke about the pilots mucking

about, and went back to talking about something else and looked forward to getting home.

An hour later we were approaching Farnborough, and the cloud cover was only about 1,000 feet. We banked, then jinxed back to the right and, out of nowhere, we nearly hit a hot-air balloon! Obviously the cloud had totally obscured it and, as we roared past, you could almost see the faces of the people standing in the basket of the balloon, staring at the plane and wondering what was going on. We were thinking much the same.

That wasn't the end of it. Instead of coming into land on the runway, we flew past at a height of about 500 feet, and I started to get a little bit concerned. Pete Boutwood, an old friend of mine who was flying home with us, had a word with the pilots and came back saying that there was indeed a problem with the plane. Remembering the difficulty we had had on the way out of Cologne, I was going to ask if it was to do with the undercarriage, but the answer presented itself almost immediately. As we were taking in Pete's words, one of the pilots came down to check that we all knew what to do in the event of a crash landing.

By then, everybody was paying attention. He told us there was a problem with the lights on the dashboard, which meant that he was not sure if the wheels were down or not. We had flown over the runway so that the control tower could take a look at our plane and tell us whether it looked as if the undercarriage was in place.

They had reported back that all looked well, but from that distance they were not completely sure. Without a proper reading from the instrument panel, the pilot couldn't be certain that our wheels had locked in place and were not going to buckle under the weight of the plane landing.

The problematic wheel was the one on the right – the others we were sure were okay – so the pilot brought us down gingerly on the left wheel first. Then he let the other side of the plane come down very gently, checking that the right wheel would hold firm. Mercifully, it did, and we got down in one piece.

"We could see the flashing lights of the fire engines and ambulances."

It was an uncomfortable feeling, and as we performed our high-speed 'wheelie' along the runway, we could see the flashing lights of the fire engines and ambulances that were waiting for us, prepared to dive in to make the rescue. In those circumstances, drivers are expected to feel less scared than most people, but this was a situation that was totally out of my control, and that I don't like. Also, I'm pretty certain that my racing car would stand up to a hefty crash, but I wasn't nearly as sure about my plane.

Once we had managed to get ourselves on to firm land, and were guzzling down the obligatory sweet tea for the occasion, I had to address the problem of getting back to Dublin. My plane was out of action for a while because of the repairs that needed to be made, so I was stranded.

Rescue appeared in the shape of some racehorse trainers who were flying their horse back to Ireland. They offered me a lift and so, in the company of some living horsepower, I got home. The only difference between me and the equine passenger was that, between us, the horse had had a better day at the races. She finished third compared to my lacklustre eighth place.

Less than a week later, I was testing in Barcelona. There was a long gap between the race at the Nurburgring and the Japanese Grand Prix, and all the teams wanted to try to make an extra push. Coming to the final corner on one of those laps, everything seemed fine. I could see Giancarlo

High risk – a pit stop

Fisichella, in a Benetton, just ahead of me and I realised that he had slowed down. Very quickly, I realised that he had slowed to a crawl and I was on target to thump the back of his car. It could have been a very nasty accident.

Instead, I took the only option that I had and went off the track to avoid Fisichella's car. At the time, I was in fourth gear, doing about 150mph, and I knew that it would hurt when my car hit the barrier. As I went in, I tried to relax, which is my normal practice in an accident, and took my hands off the wheel, because if you are tense, you will rip your muscles and do yourself no good in the process. There's no way you can resist the force, so you are better off trying to relax and enjoy the ride, taking a few mental notes along the way.

You get used to it. It might sound bizarre, but racing drivers are accustomed to having accidents, and they often talk about them as if they were the most exciting thing of all – as long as they get out in one piece.

When you know there will be an impact, there really is not an awful lot you can do other than watch what's happening with a mixture of interest and concern. There's an element of hoping it's not going to hurt, but often there isn't time to formulate a thought like that. Instead, you normally only have time to say a few choice swearwords, which I certainly managed to do that day in Barcelona.

As a racing driver, you assume that every season you will have one big crash. You hope that it won't happen, of course, but there tends to be one each year that shakes you up a little as a reminder of the danger of our job. I had

A1 Nurburgring – I chased Jacques all the way to the helipad

The tension mounts

hoped to get through 1998 without having my warning, but this was it, my biggest fright of the season. As the car went into the barrier, my helmet hit the steering wheel and my whole body was shaken up.

As I was thrown forward, I heard a fantastic 'crack' originating from somewhere under my skull. For the past year, I have been troubled by pain from the vertebrae in my neck, pain that has never been properly eased by a chiropractor, but suddenly, with that crack, it instantly felt better. The rest of me was sore, my head was aching and my knees were bruised, but the two vertebrae were fine. I have had plenty of accidents that have left me feeling bad – this was the first one that actually did me some good.

"Thankfully I only broke my collarbone instead of my neck."

Like any racing driver, I have had my fair share of shunts. I had a big crash in Formula Ford, but I blacked out and have never been able to remember a thing about it. I had a couple of pearlers on my bike as well, and I remember once landing on my head and then being thumped by the bike as it went past. Thankfully I only broke my collarbone instead of my neck.

Bikes make you particularly vulnerable, but a car is different because you are strapped inside, and when it goes out of control, it can go anywhere and do anything. A bike tends to hit the deck and go off at a tangent, but a car can go right, left, backwards, upside down, in the air. You don't know what will happen, but you're strapped inside it as an utterly helpless passenger.

After the huge crash at the first start in Belgium, Eddie Irvine said it had been terrifying 'because it just seemed to keep going on', and I know exactly how he felt. Ever since my first crash in a racing car, I have known that there is a point in any big accident when you feel like saying, 'okay, I've had enough now'. The trouble is there is always something more to come.

The worst crashes I have had are the ones where the car's suspension fails. Normally that only happens when the suspension is under maximum load, which is when the car is at its fastest speed going round the fastest corner. An accident in those circumstances will always be enough to

bring up the hairs on the back of your neck and, if you're unlucky, it's going to hurt.

I had one on the exit of the tunnel in Monaco several seasons back, where the rear suspension failed and I was very lucky not to hit anything. I went down the slip road and came to a gentle stop, thanking my lucky stars. This year, in almost exactly the same place, Alexander Wurz did the same thing, but was less lucky and bounced around all over the place. He ended up piling into a barrier, with bits of bodywork going everywhere.

If I was lucky in Monaco, then I wasn't so fortunate when my suspension failed again, this time at the exit of turn two in Estoril, in testing a few years ago, resulting in the biggest accident of my life. I was doing at least 150mph when, before I could think, the car had turned around on

me. Reduced to the status of an interested observer, I felt the car thump into a barrier on the left-hand side, going backwards, and then bounce across the track.

By now, there were no wheels on the car because they were all ripped off by the first impact. In effect, my car had been converted into a carbon-fibre sledge, and I piled into the barrier on the other side of the track just as hard. At that point, I rebounded into the middle of the track and came to a halt, with steam coming up from the car and me sitting in the cockpit counting my limbs.

You may not be surprised to know that after that I went home. I wasn't badly hurt, but I was bruised and shaken up a bit and a little concussed. My attitude was pretty much 'thank God we've got that out of the way', but it was not too long before I was back at the wheel.

You can have enormous shunts and walk away from them with barely a mark on your body. Then, at other times, you have what looks like a pretty minor shunt and it really hurts. The first time I drove on a circuit after winning my world championship in 1996 was when I went to Suzuka to do some tyre testing for Bridgestone. I had done about fifteen laps when I spun coming out of the hairpin, which is the slowest corner on the circuit, and slammed into a wall on the inside of the corner. It was only a first-gear corner, but the impact was enormous and I was seeing stars, almost knocked out, and barely noticed that my car was on fire. That was the end of that – I had gone all the way to Japan for the test, destroyed the car after half an hour and had to go home. As test sessions go, it was not exactly the perfect model.

Fear is an obstacle that is there to be overcome. It represents a form of tyranny, because if you are frightened, then you are inevitably limited by your fear from doing the things you want to do. There were times when racing was the easy part for me, and it was the public appearances and press conferences, the pressure of providing something for a big group of expectant people, that I didn't like.

Now those aspects of my life don't present a problem and, like a driving test or a school exam, I look back on my early career and can't believe I was ever frightened of something that I now enjoy so much. Like falling off a motorbike, any fear has to be confronted for the first time and, after that, you normally find it a great deal less intimidating. Without confronting your fears, you can miss out on an awful lot of life's experiences. In Monza, for instance, I struggled in qualifying and worried that I might not figure in the race, but thanks to some good tactics I came home in sixth place to add another point to the collection. Get yourself a bit of self-belief, and you can do anything . . .

'The only thing we have to fear is fear itself'

Franklin Roosevelt

'To conquer fear is the beginning of wisdom'

Bertrand Russell

'Always look on the bright side of life'

Monty Python

Chief FIA Medical Officer Professor Sid Watkins - the man I try to avoid.

There can be nowhere else on earth that is more about tomorrow than Japan. Japanese trains, motorcycles and cars are way ahead in terms of design and sophistication. If there's a way of performing a task more easily, whether it is related to work or leisure, then the Japanese have a machine that does it.

As if to underline the relentlessness of progress in Formula One, Japan provided the perfect venue for the last race. It was the end of the 1998 season, of course, but for B & H Jordan Mugen-Honda, the race was more pertinent to 1999. Everything about the trip pointed to the future.

My first task upon arriving in Japan was to visit the Mugen factory, where most of the work on our engine took place. This factory is the property of Hirotoshi Honda, the son of Soichiro Honda, who was Japan's leading industrialist after the destruction of the country in the Second World War. He was, quite simply, the man who created Honda.

Five per cent of the profits of the Honda company are provided to the Honda research and development company, which employs 7,000 scientists and engineers, some of whom are responsible for the Formula One engine programme. My visit to the factory brought home to me just how massive their resources are and left me in little doubt that, if the company's full weight was engaged to produce a Formula One engine, then Honda could propel Jordan into a championship-winning team in a very short space of time. It was quite an uplifting thought as I headed off in the Bullet Train – which makes British trains look left over from the Industrial Revolution – on my way to the Suzuka circuit, owned, incidentally, by Honda.

The thrust of our team's work in the races since Spa had been to break through from fifth place in the constructors' championship – something Jordan had not managed to do for the previous five seasons. There was a difference of only four points between us and Williams and Benetton, who were lying third and fourth, so closing such a small gap looked tantalisingly easy.

It certainly had us going. The wind tunnel was blowing non-stop throughout the five-week break after the penultimate race, at the Nurburgring, and we tested a new engine at Silverstone that Honda had built specially for Suzuka. Its specific purpose was to impress the Japanese crowd, something which is extremely important to the company.

> *"Despite everything that we were doing, scoring heavily was liable to be harder than ever."*

The reality, though, was that the race in Japan was destined to be very hard. The championship protagonists, McLaren and Ferrari, were putting in a massive effort and so were Williams, my old team, for they were determined not to lose their third place to us. Despite everything that we were doing, scoring heavily was liable to be harder than ever, but the powerful dream of joining the big boys was motivating everyone for the final race.

It was also to be Ralf's final race at Jordan. He was off to swap places with the man who had been drafted into Williams, at my expense, a couple of years before, when he was hailed as the new Michael Schumacher. In his two seasons with Williams, Heinz-Harald Frentzen recorded only one race victory and, while he was undeniably quick on occasion, he never really lived up to the hype that had persuaded Frank Williams to sign him up in the first place.

What all this meant for Suzuka was that in the final round Ralf and Heinz-Harald would both be expected to give their best to defeat the very teams for whom they would be driving the following year – surely a severe test of a driver's loyalty and political integrity if ever there was one.

Eddie Jordan and Mr Honda plan ahead

The great Suzuka

Honda escape mechanism

Ours was the sub-plot to the main event of the weekend, Mika Hakkinen versus Michael Schumacher, but it was no less important to us for that. The showdown between the two contenders really only extended to qualifying, though, because, after knocking the wind out of Mika fairly comprehensively by grabbing pole position, Michael then threw it away by stalling on the grid, albeit after the first start had also been aborted.

Few people can imagine what it must have been like for Mika to have all the build-up to the beginning of the race instantaneously snatched away by an aborted start – twice! For me, in 1996, it had only happened once, and I thought that was cruel enough, but the consolation for Mika this time was that, in the third attempt at getting the race going, his only rival was going to be at the back of the grid.

I played hard but
fair with Michael

Getting to know you – me and Heinz-Harald Frentzen

After all the drama of qualifying, all the pre-race strategic planning, all the effort and money spent on a special engine, tyres and so on, the clash of the titans was now a demonstration run for McLaren. Michael got to show off his talent for overtaking, but at the same time he knew that his task was now almost impossible. If he passed all the other cars, he would still have to beat Mika by four points and, even for Michael, that was not going to be easy.

As it transpired, it was a forlorn hope, because his tyre burst and ended his race, but he passed quite a few cars in a very short space of time – until he caught up with me. I was having a vital and bitter battle to stay in contention with the Williams cars of Jacques and Heinz-Harald, who were just in front of me, and this was important. I was barely in the points, but not by enough for us to beat Benetton in the constructors' championship. We needed to score two points. Ralf was out with a blown engine, caused by the overheating it suffered in all the re-starts, so everything was down to me.

I had no desire to stop Michael challenging for a third world crown. Contrary to the popular and understandable belief that I have some kind of revenge motive against him for things in the past, I would never want to spoil a show-down for the world championship. If I had backed off to let him past, two things would have been conceded: a point-scoring position, and any opportunity of passing Jacques for the next few laps. In that situation, my loyalty was to B & H Jordan Mugen-Honda, and I could not help the fact that Michael had had to start from the back.

Bridgestones all round for 1999

The unique Tazio Nuvolari

Ralf and I
get on with it

I do not consider it my obligation to stand aside for any-body in a straight race and, as far as I was concerned, I did absolutely nothing wrong. I think Michael realised that, this time, he could have no legitimate gripe, but that didn't stop him. After Ralf had claimed, falsely, that Eddie Jordan had come on to the radio three times to get me to move over for his brother, Michael later suggested that I had a fixation about him – a kind of Schu fetish. I had to make an early pit-stop anyway, and after that he progressed unhindered by me until he went out. I guess it was just not one of his lucky days.

Meanwhile, things were getting pretty exciting for us Jordan lot, because I was running fifth and having one of my best races of the year. The pressure was relentless all race long, with Jacques behind while I was harrying Heinz-Harald for all I was worth. We were going at it hammer and tongs, and he was no doubt mindful that, although we are going to be team-mates next year, he still had to finish off his commitment to the team who no longer wanted him. Racing drivers in the thick of a race, though, are uninfluenced by the colour of their cars. All that matters is being in front of the other guy.

Having deposed Jacques earlier, caught up again with Heinz-Harald and then pressured him for fifty-three laps of one of the toughest circuits in the world, I was not going to pass up an opportunity if one arose, and it came on the last lap. Heinz-Harald thought he had fourth place in the bag and eased off just a little too soon. I saw a gap braking into the final corner of the season and went for it. It was one of my best passes since overtaking Michael Schumacher to lead in Hungary in 1997 and, like that day in Budapest, I'm afraid to say that ITV missed it. In Hungary, they went to a commercial break at the wrong moment and, I suppose with all the hullabaloo about Mika's success (which was entirely justified and I completely en-dorse), my final fling in Japan went unnoticed – even, in fact, by Eddie Jordan.

He, like most of the team, was alerted to the moment by Ian Phillips, Jordan's commercial director, who was glued faithfully to one of the monitors on the pit-wall. When he saw me, all four tyres smoking and half the car on the grass, slithering past Heinz-Harald, he screamed in hor-ror, thinking that Jordan's priceless record move up to fourth in the constructors' championship was about to be dumped into the gravel trap. You see, I didn't actually need to pass Frentzen for us to beat Benetton, but nobody had told me that, so I wasn't going to leave anything to chance! Ah well, you try your best.

Needless to say, the whole Jordan team were as pleased as punch. It was a great way to end what had been a

> "Things were getting pretty exciting for us Jordan lot, because I was running fifth and having one of my best races of the year."

remarkable season – no points halfway through the year transformed into the best season the team has ever had, including that priceless gem in Spa.

The future looks even brighter. 1999 is already on our minds, beckoning like a holiday brochure. The race never ends, you see. Hardly dry from his champagne soaking on the podium, Mika talked of winning back-to-back championships. Then everyone stayed on for two more days of testing in Suzuka to try out the new Bridgestone tyres, designed with the four grooves that 1999 regulations demand. Michael promised to start work immediately on his new Ferrari and the winter testing programme slid seamlessly into gear. It's non-stop: non-stop testing, non-stop dreaming, non-stop travelling, non-stop competition, non-stop pressure, non-stop excitement.

"The future looks even brighter. 1999 is already on our minds, beckoning like a holiday brochure."

But when do I stop? I have to stop some time. I ended 1998 as a thirty-eight-year-old, the oldest driver on the grid. The sad old man of Formula One? No, not sad, and I don't think age is a factor as much as a love of what you do. Tazio Nuvolari was thirty-eight when he became a full-time car racer, because before that he had raced bikes. He is still regarded as one of the greatest drivers ever.

Last start of 1998

Heinz-Harald Frentzen will partner me in 1999

But time is the factor we all fight against in Formula One, and inevitably time wins. I suppose I should be grateful that I am in a sport that enables me to compete up to what is comparatively a high age limit. If I was a tennis player or footballer, a skier or swimmer, it would be time now for other things, but driving is a skill that requires a blend of touch, reactions, concentration, experience and fitness.

If it was all about reactions, concentration and touch, then I suppose you could liken it to playing the piano. At what age is a concert pianist at his or her height? At what age will Gary Kasparov lose his ability to concentrate? John Glenn has gone back into space, so he obviously can't kick the habit.

In my case, the only criteria for deciding how long I continue racing will be my level of competitiveness and whether I am happy doing it, which all boils down to a single question – can I still win?

In 1998 I won, and I held my own against a team-mate fifteen years my junior. Next season, B & H Jordan Mugen-Honda will have better equipment and I believe we will be very competitive. That motivates me. We all worked hard to make 1998 a success from a dismal start and, if we can do it again in 1999, anything could be possible.

Racing has given me everything. I have been to my personal outer limits and found out more about myself than I ever could have believed possible. It has made me stronger and wiser, and it has certainly made me richer. I know who my real friends are and, without them, I might never have achieved a fifth of whatever I have done. If I could have another shot at the world title, I would love it, but I know I don't need that to be happy. I just want to be able to say I have done my best.

The future? No, don't tell me what happens. I want to find out for myself.

Hill team-mate's joint number one status

A *Little, Brown* Book

First published in Great Britain in 1998
by Little, Brown and Company
This paperback edition published in 1999
by Little, Brown and Company
Text copyright © 1998 Damon Hill
All photographs by Keith Sutton copyright © Sutton Motorsport Images
with the following exceptions:-
pages 30–1 Patrick Vinet/page 73 Popperfoto/pages 74, 107, 108–9,
110, 185 Phipps Photographic/page 128 Sporting Pictures UK Ltd/
pages 129, 134 Peter Egmond/pages 172–3 Flavio Mazzi/pages
216-7 Central Press Photo Ltd.

The moral right of the author has been asserted.

A CIP catalogue record for this book is available from the British Library.

ISBN 0 316 85392 5

Designed by Peter Boutwood
Layout by The Bridgewater Book Company
Printed in Italy by EuroGrafica/L.E.G.O. S.p.A.

Little, Brown and Company (UK)
Brettenham House
Lancaster Place
London WC2E 7EN

Acknowledgements

There are plenty of people who helped me to complete this book, but
I especially want to thank my wife Georgie and our children, Oliver,
Joshua, Tabatha and Rosie, who have all put up with my writer's tempera-
ment; to Pete Boutwood and Michael Breen, for helping me to keep my
mind on the job; to everybody at Jordan, for helping me to do the job
in the first place; to Benson & Hedges, for making the car yellow; to
Little, Brown, for making this book appear; to Keith Sutton, for making
me appear in the book; and to Adam Parsons, who pestered me to
death and made my ramblings intelligible.

– *Damon Hill, November 1998*